Activities for Task-Based Learning

Integrating a fluency first approach
into the ELT classroom

Neil Anderson and Neil McCutcheon

DELTA Publishing

Dedication and acknowledgements

We would like to dedicate this book to our friend and mentor, Steve Oakes.
We'd also like to thank all the students and trainees who have willingly
participated in and given feedback on our ideas.
Neil Anderson would above all like to thank Katy, Alex and Leo for their
unwavering patience and support.
Thank you as well to our patient editor.

Download the free DELTA Augmented app onto your device	Start picture recognition and scan the pages with this icon	Download files and use them now or save them for later

1st edition 1 54321 | 2023 22 21 20 19

The last figure shown denotes the year of impression.

DELTA Publishing, 2019

www.deltapublishing.co.uk
www.klett-sprachen.de/delta

© Ernst Klett Sprachen GmbH, Rotebühlstraße 77, 70178 Stuttgart, 2019

Authors: Neil Anderson, Neil McCutcheon
Series Editor: Jason Anderson
Cover and layout: Andreas Drabarek
Design: bostext OHG, D-71292 Friolzheim
Printing and binding: Salzland Druck, Staßfurt

ISBN 978-3-12-501701-6

Preface

It is now 40 years since N.S. Prabhu began his innovative research into task-based language teaching in Bangalore, India. Since then, task-based learning (TBL) has become established as one of the best-known and most researched approaches within the communicative language teaching movement, and supported by a number of prominent theorists and researchers in the second language acquisition literature (notably Rod Ellis, Michael Long and Peter Skehan). Yet, despite the plethora of research on TBL, and the theoretical arguments offered in support of it, it is notable how few practical resources exist to support teachers interested in experimenting with TBL in their own classrooms. For this reason, **Activities for Task-Based Learning** is a very welcome addition to the teacher's library, one that I suspect will become a well-thumbed favourite in staff rooms around the world.

As they point out in their introduction to the book, the authors adopt a 'wider conception' of TBL without overlooking the sometimes complex theory that underpins it. As well as many activities that would fall under the narrower definitions of 'real world' tasks argued for by Long (2015), **Activities for Task-Based Learning** also includes a range of classroom practice activities that nonetheless 'allow the learners to flex their communicative muscles', as the authors put it, using language *meaningfully* and for *communicative* purposes, a key intention of Prabhu's original work (1987). **Activities for Task-Based Learning** includes a structural index to allow teachers who work within the constraints of a grammar syllabus (common in many parts of the world) to make use of the activities through what Ellis has called 'focused tasks' – tasks designed to practise a specific language point. These have been shown to lead to significant learning when used within a 'task-supported' approach to language teaching (Li, Ellis & Zhu, 2016), comparing favourably even to unfocused tasks of the kind that Long (2015) argues for.

Perhaps the biggest challenge in writing a books of tasks for the classroom, a challenge that the authors have, in my opinion, met well, is to compile tasks that do not prescribe a single language structure, but allow for students to interact meaningfully to complete the tasks using structures at different levels of proficiency (see their discussion of **5a Nostalgia story** in the Introduction). The key advantage of such activities for us teachers is their flexibility – we can keep coming back to them again and again, from intermediate to advanced levels of proficiency, meaning they become staples among practitioner communities.

I look forward to trying out some of the tasks in **Activities for Task-Based Learning** in my own classroom, and thank the authors heartily for their contribution to the DELTA Publishing Ideas in Action series!

Jason Anderson
Series Editor: Ideas in Action

Activities for Task-Based Learning

				Page
0	**Introduction to task-based learning**		Brief history, key principles, research evidence for task-based learning, implementing task-based learning in your classroom.	7
1	**Micro-strategies and tools**		Micro-strategies and tools for pre-task, on-task and post-task lesson phases.	18
2	**Categorising**	*Levels of example activities*	Activities include listing, grouping, sorting, ranking.	30
	2a Crime and punishment	B1+	From a list of crimes, students rank according to seriousness and decide on appropriate sentences.	30
	2b Domestic robot	A2–B2	Students brainstorm chores they dislike and prioritise which "apps" to install.	33
	2c Dangerous animals	A2–B2	Students rank animals according to how dangerous they are, check against fact files and review their choices.	36
	2d Me not me	All	Students categorise a topic according to a personal association.	40
	2e My neighbourhood	B1–C1	Students list and compare good and bad aspects of where they live.	43
	2f Speed flatmates	A2–C1	Students list characteristics of good / bad flatmates then do a "speed-dating" activity to find good matches.	47
3	**Opinion gaps**	*Levels of example activities*	Activities include comparing and evaluating opinions and experiences.	50
	3a How strict were your parents?	B1+	Students answer a questionnaire and decide who had the strictest parents.	50
	3b Polarities + Opinion gallery	A2–C2	Students form groups, brainstorm against a topic, then face off and debate.	53
	3c Counsellors / Dilemmas	A2+	Role play in which students write down a problem or dilemma, and talk to other students in role as counsellors.	57
	3d Tenancy agreement	A2+	Students decide on tenant and landlord needs, before pairing off to reach and record agreements.	59
	3e This house believes …	B1–C2	Students choose a topic for debate, then prepare a case in groups. Examples: *Things are meant to be* v *pure chance*. The benefits of social media outweigh the disadvantages.	62

				Page
3f	FutureTech	A2–B2	Students discuss given examples of potential future technology and decide how likely, useful and dangerous they would be.	65
3g	Changes	A2–B2	Students find out who has changed the most over a period of time.	69
4	**Problem-solving**	*Levels of example activities*	Activities include identifying, analyzing and solving problems.	72
4a	Team problem-solving	A2 +	Students listen to two versions of a story as a jigsaw listening, and collaborate in order to decide what action to take.	72
4b	Fake News!	B1 +	Students read internet articles and decide which one is fake and which are (largely) true.	76
4c	Pictures and lies	A1–B1	Based on a theme, three students are given a picture, one a blank; the other students interview them in turn and determine who has the blank.	80
4d	Identity swap	A2 +	Students answer questions as someone else in the class and then compare to see if they were right. (Variation: Profiles activity for new classes.)	83
5	**Sharing personal experiences**	*Levels of example activities*	Activities include opportunities for students to share and explore something personal to them.	85
5a	Nostalgia story	A2–B2	Students recall a happy period of their life and share / ask about it.	85
5b	Talking about a song	B1–B2 +	Mini-presentation - Students explain the lyric to a song and why it's important to them.	88
5c	Where were you when…?	A2 +	Students recount where they were when important world events took place. Variation: draw your partner's timeline.	91
5d	My life in apps	B1 +	Students share the apps on their smartphones that say something about their identity.	94
5e	Heroes	B1–C2	Mini-presentation. Students nominate someone they admire for an award e.g. "ultimate icon" or most important person in a particular field. Class votes.	97
5f	Happy accidents	B2 +	Students talk about how their lives would be different in the light of counterfactuals. Begin with teacher's example.	99
5g	Folk remedies	A2 +	Students talk about what they do to prevent / treat common ailments such as colds, flu, hiccups and report back.	102
5h	Cook-off	A2 +	Competition in which students create recipes and vote for their favourites in a group, or the whole class.	104

				Page
6	**Creative (design) tasks**	*Levels of example activities*	Activities include opportunities to combine the imagination with personal experience to create something.	107
	6a	Introducing the band	A2–B2	Interview role-play: Students take on the roles of members of a fantasy band - and journalists.	107
	6b	Home exchange	A2–B2	Students draw a plan of their flat/ house or one they know well. Mingle and find a tenant.	110
	6c	Soundtracks	B1–C2	Students listen to excerpts from movie soundtracks, design and pitch their movie based on it.	113
	6d	Rate your stay	B1+	Students respond to a stimulus of a bad hotel and write a review, then read and evaluate each others' reviews.	116
	6e	Struggling artist	A1+	Students draw their masterpiece, then create a gallery to admire and interpret the work of their peers.	120
	6f	Elevator pitch	B1–C2	Students have a personal project, or something for their community. They compete for patrons.	122
7	**Whole class**			Activities where students work together as a whole class to solve a shared problem or complete a task.	125
	7a	Dictogloss	A2–C1	Short text read aloud, students reconstruct. Versions compared.	126
	7b	Decon-Recon	A1+	Text is deconstructed into fact sentences then later reconstructed. Versions compared.	129
	7c	Retranslation	B1+	Short text translated from English into L1, later translated back. Versions compared.	132
	7d	Text recon	B1–B2	Students given title and key words in order, then reconstruct the story. Versions compared.	134
	7e	Story jigsaw	B1–C2	Students reconstruct a story based on the first sentence and a chance to interrogate the teacher.	137
	Additional resources				142
	Glossary of key terms				146
	Index of language areas				149
	References				150

Scan this symbol 📖 to download the audio recordings.

You can find transcripts of the audio recordings on our website: **deltapublishing.co.uk**

Introduction to task-based learning

Education, including language education, has become ever more student-centred over the past five decades. These changes have followed research findings about child and adult language development, cognitive processes and motivation. In language teaching, we now understand much more than we did about the natural developmental processes referred to as language acquisition, both as regards the learning of a first and second (or subsequent) language. In the pedagogical literature, one approach that is robustly supported by research is task-based learning (TBL), which is referred to in the literature on Second Language Acquisition as task-based language teaching (TBL).

TBL has been one ingredient in various course materials, but there has always been a lack of a single go-to resource both for varied and motivating classroom tasks, and for practical tips regarding teachers' interventions. We decided to write this book in order to address this need. It provides a collection of meaningful tasks, and offers suggestions both about specific "emergent" language that might arise during tasks, and about how this language might best be captured and put to use.

1. A brief history of task-based language teaching

The beginnings of a genuinely task-based approach in ELT are usually traced to N.S. Prabhu's Bangalore Project on which he worked between 1979 and 1984. This project was seminal because, in order to make English lessons appeal to the young people in the state secondary schools for which he was responsible for overseeing, Prabhu chose tasks as the basis of his syllabus, rather than the structural approach current at the time. He admits that he did this as a deliberate attempt to put principles into practice and reported his findings in his book Second Language Pedagogy (1987). The fact that the approach became so widely known in the mainstream of ELT is largely due to the work of Jane and Dave Willis in writing and presenting about TBL, beginning with the seminal **A Framework For Task-Based Learning** (1996). More recently, Mike Long has summed up an immense amount of scholarship relevant to TBL in his 2015 book **Second Language Acquisition and Task-Based Language Teaching**. At the same time there has been a steady growth in the number of coursebooks, both in general English and in ELT for specific contexts, which have included tasks as a key feature of each teaching unit, though conspicuously without using these as an organising principle.

What is a task?

A task-based syllabus puts the **achievement of communicative tasks** at the centre of what students have to do in the classroom. The easiest way to define a task is that it is something that students do as part of their everyday lives, and for which they need the second language. Tasks should be **purposeful**, and engage your students in **real communication**, by which we mean that other **participants** in the tasks will **have a genuine reason to listen** to whoever is speaking.

> A task is something that students do as part of their everyday lives…
> Tasks should be purposeful and engage your students in real communication…

For the purpose of this book, we take a wide view of what a task can be – from participating in a job interview to giving a short presentation; from playing a game to designing parts of an advertising campaign. We hope that the tasks will also be engaging on a personal level, and fun.

Examples of classroom tasks with which readers may already be familiar are:

- versions of a well-known activity **Alibi**, in which students have to invent a story which will "match" as closely as possible with that of a partner to prove (under close questioning) they were not present at an imaginary crime scene;
- classroom surveys, in which students generate questions and poll the class in order to find who, for example, are the biggest shopaholics or the most health-conscious people in the class;
- an activity where students draw a time-line based on the important events in their lives, and then in pairs complete a blank time-line for a partner based on the events they are told about. They then look for similarities between their life stories.

2. Key principles of task-based learning

- TBL is a **student-centred** pedagogy. It is based on the belief that language learning should be helping students to say (better) what they want to say in English. Meaning is primary. Students are not given other people's meanings to regurgitate. Instead, a task encourages students to share *their* opinions; *their* experiences; *their* solutions to problems. Skehan, P. (2004).

> ... the best tasks ... necessitate communication; students work together to reach a concrete outcome, such as solving a problem, comparing experiences, or creating something.

- TBL **prioritises meaning** because this is what language is ultimately *for*. It is important to make the distinction between meaning things in English, and simply rehearsing grammar structures, for whatever else the communicative approach may be, it is precisely this conception of language that is at its core.
- **Accuracy develops out of fluency** and not the other way round: TBL is a **fluency first** approach. This has also been described by Patsy Lightbown and Nina Spada as a "get it right in the end" approach, and elsewhere as *using* a language in order to *learn* it – rather than the obverse! This approach holds that language is best learned within the context of communicative events because it is through having to manipulate language forms in order to express personal meanings that these forms become salient, and in the end memorable, for students. **Fluency-based stages**, which many teachers think of as the most engaging part of lessons, **come early on in the timeline of the lesson**. The focus on specific language forms comes later. Teaching is most effective when the teacher follows the students' lead by attending to and providing feedback on **emergent language**.
- Tasks are **social and physical**. This is because language is profoundly social. Of particular importance in language acquisition are the interactions between students themselves; between the students and the teacher who is able to "scaffold" the learning process; and between the student and the wider linguistic community that she is seeking to be a part of. A more radical but entirely plausible view is that, in addition to this, language is actually embodied; paralinguistic features such as facial expressions are an essential part of communication. Watching people gesturing frantically while talking on a handless phone set to someone who can't see them offers evidence for this. (For a discussion of this idea, see Thornbury, S. 2013.) This is why the best tasks are designed in such a way that they necessitate communication; students work together to reach a concrete outcome, such as solving a problem, comparing experiences, or creating something.

> "A presentation methodology is based on the belief that out of accuracy comes fluency. A task-based methodology is based on the belief that out of fluency comes accuracy, and that learning is prompted and refined by the need to communicate." Willis D. (1990) The Lexical Syllabus in Scott Thornbury's **30 Language Teaching Methods** (2017: 64)

For example, in our **5a Nostalgia story** task, students first prepare and then share stories about past experiences; they are then exposed through a teacher model to the range of forms they could have used (including ones they may not have e.g. *used to / would* for past habit), and analyse these, before preparing to repeat their stories with a new partner, and with more attention to the use of a wider variety of forms. (A pre-intermediate student may now try to incorporate *used to* into their repertoire; an upper intermediate may now try to incorporate *would* into theirs.)

- All this means that tasks should ideally be **authentic**. There ought to be some **relationship between a task and real-world activities**, whether this is more instrumental (e.g. a job interview) or more functional (e.g. comparing, listing, evaluating) – see the list of communicative situations below in section 3.

What about grammar?

We realise that the reality of much teaching is that most teachers operate with a course book with a **structure-based syllabus**, and that many students expect lessons to have a focus on discrete items. For the benefit of these teachers, **we have provided with each task a list of language items** (grammar, vocabulary, functional exponents) which are likely to arise as students do the tasks, and ideas about how and when to focus on language. Note that the tasks are cross-referenced to a list of the most common language items in the index. (NB the language items accompanying each task are meant as a guide and are not supposed to be exhaustive.)

Meanwhile, the advantage (for the busy teacher) is that, precisely because they are not primarily structure-based, the tasks here can be easily adapted for different levels. A teacher who re-uses any of the tasks will gain from this experience as they become more familiar with the language items that emerge naturally during the task performance. (See **emergent language** in the glossary.)

3. How do I choose tasks for my learning context?

In ELT, there has been some controversy about what constitutes a task for teaching purposes, as writers see different aspects as being essential.

According to what we might call a narrow conception of TBL, the tasks set for the students must be decided after a process of in-depth needs analysis. By means of questionnaires, an analysis of the contexts in which they need to use English, and standardised tests, students' subjective needs (as they perceive them) and objective needs (determined by the situations in which they need to use English) are identified. The menu of tasks will then reflect as much as possible how the students need to use the language for their purposes. It is hard to disagree with the pedagogic principles at work here – an ideal menu of tasks would be free from coursebook materials, and once sequenced in terms of perceived difficulty, this would constitute the syllabus in its own right.

Some examples of how language is used in natural communicative situations, referred to in discourse theory as **functions**, are:

- asking questions
- reporting an event in the past
- talking about the way one used to be
- talking about future plans
- comparing and contrasting. See Finocchiaro, M., Brumfit, C. (1983)

Differing from this narrow view is a wider conception of tasks, briefly mentioned above. This includes the kind of pedagogic tasks that have been mentioned – that is, various classroom activities (games, role-plays, interviews, "speed-dating" etc.) which, despite not being drawn directly from real world contexts such as business and academic life, nonetheless resemble real-life situations and allow the students to flex their communicative muscles. (Incidentally, it's worth noting that Prabhu's conception of tasks was even wider, including both rule-focused and form-focused activities!)

"The games (s) play, the problems they solve, the experiences they share, may or may not be the things that they will do in real life, but their use of language, because it is purposeful and real, will replicate features of language use outside the classroom." Willis & Willis (1996)

While we are aware that this is a compromise position, we have ensured that the tasks remain emphatically student-centred in that they are fun, communicative, and relevant to students' needs. Many of them reflect the kind of functions listed above. They all enable students to produce a wide variety of language forms in the performance of the task, and these language forms can be focused on after the task in various ways – or not at all, if you are uncomfortable with the idea of explicit language instruction.

Finally, as part of each task, we have included short sections on how to vary the subject matter or the design. This is so that you can match tasks as far as possible to the interests and language needs of your particular students.

4. Research evidence supporting a task-based approach

"What we know about language learning strongly suggests the primacy of meaning negotiation supported by a focus on form, as proposed by TBLT."
Klapper, J., & Rees , (2003). Reviewing the case for explicit grammar instruction in the university foreign language learning context. Language Teaching Research, 7(3), 285–314.

From Mike Long – Long M., **In Defense of Tasks and TBLT: Nonissues and Real Issues**, *Annual Review of Applied Linguistics,* 36 (2016) CUP

As pointed out in the introductory section above, task-based language teaching is well supported by research findings from **Second Language Acquisition (SLA).** This is largely because it primarily **learner-driven** in terms of the language which arises – that is, it follows the **student's "internal syllabus"** rather than the pre-determined syllabus of a book publisher. Ever since Larry Selinker introduced the key concept of **interlanguage** in 1972, teachers have been made aware of the existence of (more or less) fixed developmental sequences in language acquisition. Researchers have always disagreed about the value of instruction, but an important consensus emerges: instruction can expedite the acquisition process, but appears to do little to alter the sequence in which structures are acquired.

Related to this is the fact that TBL engages both the conscious and unconscious processes at work in language learning, and allows plenty of scope for the unconscious processes to operate, which seem to be more involved in learning than they are sometimes given credit for.

"Instruction is successful which recruits temporary episodes of explicit learning as an aid to subsequent implicit processing."

Mike Long, **Second Language Acquisition and Task-Based Language Teaching** (2015) p.50

In the history of SLA research, a distinction is frequently drawn between **implicit** and **explicit learning**. The former is, according to Mike Long, "learning without awareness of what is learned" and can often occur **incidentally,** that is, when the student is paying attention to something else, and simply attends to words and structures as they arise in context, rather than focusing on them consciously outside the stream of communication. Because this is the way we learn our first language, it must be true that the overwhelming majority of language learning happens in this way; Long calls it the "default process".

Explicit learning, by contrast, is **intentional** and conscious. This is the kind of learning that happens in typical classroom situations when second (or first) language students are asked to focus on certain structures or vocabulary items; commit words and phrases to memory; and engage in accuracy-focused practice.

The relationship between implicit and explicit learning in second language acquisition is still not wholly understood. According to Rod Ellis (2015: 285-288) the combination of both appears to be a good thing. This is because the two types of learning help students to develop *implicit* knowledge of language, which is the type needed in situations where students are called upon to be fluent. Of course, instruction will certainly add to a student's explicit knowledge, which enables accuracy in situations where a more careful style is required, for example in examinations. Recent research suggests that the effects of implicit learning may be longer lasting.

In the weaker version of communicative language teaching that has come to dominate much of the ELT industry, grammatical syllabuses, which prioritise explicit learning, never really lost their hold probably because they are easier for publishers to package and sequence. Doing more TBL in class will help to redress the balance between the two types of learning, since the tasks clearly provide plenty of opportunity at different points in the cycle for implicit learning, while not neglecting an explicit focus on language. Furthermore, a teacher following a more task-based approach need not impose any artificial sequence of structures; judging the challenge level inherent in the task itself is all that is required.

In her 1996 book, Jane Willis cites the following factors as being important features of good tasks: exposure, motivation, use and instruction

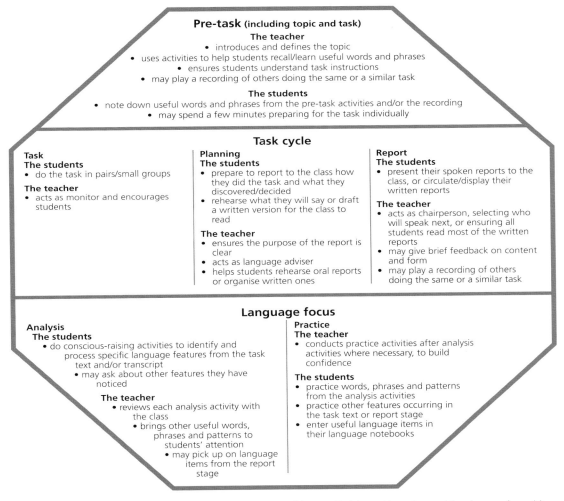

Willis, J. 1996. A framework for task-based learning. For more recent ideas on Task-based Learning and free lesson plans visit www.willis-elt.co.uk and see Willis, D. and Willis, J. 2007. Doing Task-based Teaching. Oxford University Press. For the theories behind this Framework, see Willis, D. and Willis, J. 2010.
'Six propositions in search of a methodology: applying linguistics to task-based language teaching' in S. Hunston & D. Oakey (eds) *Introducing Applied Linguistics: Concepts and Skills* Routledge.

a) Exposure

> "Anything that increases the amount of exposure, use, time or attention to vocabulary is likely to increase learning." (Schmidt, 2008, in **Nation, Learning Vocabulary in Another Language**, 2013: 102)

The case for the benefits of exposing language learners to a large amount of language is uncontroversial.

The argument for the **importance of exposure (also called comprehensible input)** to language acquisition has of course been made most consistently by Stephen Krashen, and in the past decade, ISP Nation and Michael Hoey have both argued that acquiring a range of vocabulary, including how to use this, depends on repeated exposure to lexical items, and this is best if the items are encountered in an authentic context. All this is equally true of structures. In the task cycle, seen above, there is exposure to language throughout, but it especially through the use of texts (short articles, recordings) and teachers' models of tasks in the pre-task phase of the cycle that students will be exposed to good quality language, including **authentic** language. For this reason, we have included short recordings and written text with certain tasks in this book, such as the fact files in the tasks **3e FutureTech** and **2c Dangerous animals**. These may be used just as they are, or may prompt teachers with ideas for their own texts. In addition, students will get useful input in plenary stages, when students report back to the whole class.

b) Use

Exposure to the language is not sufficient to bring about a good command of the language (at native and near-native levels) and therefore must be balanced by **opportunities for output**. Being in communicative situations, unmediated by an instructor, but where students must **negotiate meaning,** forces them to pay attention in many cases to formal structures in the language. This idea is mostly associated with Mike Long's Interaction Hypothesis, developed in the 1980s.

Having practice opportunities helps to make these structures – especially more complex ones – automatic, and also helps students to develop an explicit awareness of when to use them.

There are opportunities for students to use language naturally throughout the task cycle, primarily of course to do the tasks themselves, but also in a more careful style in the **reporting back (content feedback)** stage that follows. It is at these moments that students will, at first independently of the teacher, have the opportunity to focus on form, because they offer affordances for feedback from other students (during the task).

There are also opportunities for discussion in the pre-task stage, and we have drawn the reader's attention to these wherever they arise – for example, the controversial judicial decision in **2a Crime and punishment**.

> "The responses that learners receive when meaning is negotiated… delivers feedback to the learner at the most propitious moment. The feedback arises when meaning is problematic, and when the learner is thought to be most receptive. In addition, it is likely to be personalised, since… what will happen naturally will be the provision of useful information on precisely the area of language that the learner is struggling with."
>
> (Skehan, 2003 Task-Based Instruction in **Language Teaching 36** here reporting the findings of Long – and Pica, 1994)

c) Motivation

The role of affect in language learning has been recognised as important in Communicative Language Teaching at least since the late 1960s. From the work of scholars such as Carl Rogers, Earl Stevick and Zoltan Dörnyei, we know that affective factors are among the greatest predictors of success in a second language. Teachers understand that enjoyment of lessons is not an "add-on" but something that will likely lead to more autonomous learning, multiplying the opportunities for exposure and language use – through independent study and extra-curricular engagement with the L2 community, face to face or online.

Dave Willis mentions that one reason why studying language through tasks is motivating is because it has a "high surrender value", i.e. with only a few lessons, they will have developed confidence with communicating in the language, albeit with inaccuracies. (Willis, Dave & Jane 2007:31)

In addition, if tasks are intrinsically motivating, students are more likely to enter that enviable state of "flow" that happens when one is absorbed in something that is optimally challenging, being neither too easy nor too difficult. This is the kind of feeling that seasoned runners describe, or that rises in an experienced musician improvising on stage – or in a child constructing a sand castle. Flow is often cited in motivational and self-help manuals as being not just a stepping stone on the road to happiness, but constitutive of it. (Csikszentmihaly, Mihaly)

We believe that language learning should be a happy experience wherever possible, and to this end we have dedicated sections for tasks to do with sharing personal information; creative tasks; and problems to solve, which we hope will be intrinsically motivating and enjoyable, especially when adapted with the interests of particular students in mind.

d) Instruction

This is where the students' attention is drawn explicitly to features of the language.

In case there was any doubt about the value of L2 instruction, Norris & Ortega, (2000) in a **meta-analysis** of studies into language acquisition, concluded that:
- it makes a difference.
- the observed effect is substantial.
- explicit types of instruction can be more successful than implicit types of instruction.

One well-known estimate for how much of a language course should be dedicated to explicit instruction is 25%. See Nation, I.S.P. (2013).

"For most learners, the use of feedback may constitute the most potent source of improvement in target language development." Chaudron (1988) in **Second Language Classrooms: Research on teaching and learning**.

The teacher may provide some formative feedback during the task (i.e. on-the-spot correction and vocabulary support) and is strongly encouraged to provide more deliberate, focused feedback on student language in the latter phases of the cycle, which is a dedicated language-focused stage.

5. How and when should the teacher focus on language?

Feedback on students' language can include both peer feedback and the targeted expert feedback from the teacher. The attempt to create, or formalise, the "aha!" moments that occur during the performance of tasks is known as **focus on form (FonF).**

For decades, it has been accepted as important that the form focus is linked closely to meaning. Patsy Lightbown notes that Focus on Form is more likely to be effective "at the moment when students know what they want to say, indeed are trying to say something, and the means to say it more correctly is offered to them". Obviously, within a fluency-first approach, there are plenty of opportunities for this to happen. Very often the FonF takes the form of reactive **recasts** – on-the-spot corrected or upgraded reformulations of what a student is trying to say.

> e.g. Student: "The stage was destructed."
> Teacher: "Really? Was it completely destroyed?"

According to Mike Long (2015: 55) these recasts are effective because
- they are immediately relevant to what students are trying to say.
- there is a joint attentional focus on the message, and the language "code".
- the student's attentional resources have been freed up, the message having been delivered.
- the student is invested in the exchange; it is relevant for her.

These explicit teaching moments, while they share several features of conventional clarification, are different in several important ways. The focus is often reactive, rather than pre-determined, and will typically deal with a range of items, rather than being restricted to one limited grammatical focus. These interventions will often be short.

> "A key characteristic of focus on form, negative feedback, and **expansions** of various kinds, however, is that they are reactive, supplied in harmony with a learner's current developmental readiness to learn." Long M., In **Defense of Tasks and TBLT: Nonissues and Real Issues**, *Annual Review of Applied Linguistics,* 36 (2016)

In the case of a task such as **3a How strict were your parents?** the focus on the anticipated emergent language (verb complementation: *make, let, allow, force, encourage, ask, tell, want somebody (to)*+ V; and vocabulary *be allowed to* etc.) could come initially with the questionnaire, and in more depth after the teacher/proficient speaker's model, later on in the sequence.

In the task **7b Decon-Recon**, the focus on language comes when students compare their version of the deconstructed text with the original – this comparison between their version and the target model is said to promote **noticing** of linguistic gaps between their output and the target model. See Long M. (2015).

6. How can a more lexical teaching approach be included?

"The teaching of lexis and grammar should serve communication, hence language learning should be about learning to perform real world communicative tasks through a range of high frequency L2 chunks and constructions." (Gianfranco Conti, retrieved from https://gianfrancoconti.wordpress.com/ on 20.09.18)

It is not the purpose of this book to outline in depth the benefits of a more lexical approach to language teaching; this has been done admirably well, including recently in **Teaching Lexically** by Hugh Dellar and Andrew Walkley, in the DELTA Publishing Teacher Development Series. A brief introduction to this approach will be enough to show how tasks lend themselves to lexical teaching, especially helping students' ability to produce **appropriate** utterances in typical situations.

It is now universally accepted that fluent speakers are able to make use of a vast lexical store of easily accessible, unanalysed **"chunks"** of formulaic language. Indeed, we only depart from this when we have to – in order to construct original meanings. By involving learners in typical communicative situations in this book, such as in the tasks **4a Bad neighbours** and **3d Tenancy agreement**, we encourage students and teachers to make use of such formulaic sequences, and to focus on lexical chunks in feedback and clarification stages.

Participating in the kind of situations mentioned above allows students to have feedback and expansion on appropriate lexis, including functional **sentence stems,** which are listed together with relevant grammatical structures in the **language feedback options** sections following each task.

Note that the cognitive demands at each stage of a task's performance can be adjusted so as to allow the learners the opportunity to draw on their automatic lexical store, or to focus more carefully on accuracy, which can happen following the main task when learners work together to produce a report for the class. This slowing down of the task, building in preparation time, allows for more **syntactic complexity.** Conversely, a task segment that has to be done under time constraints will force learners to be more fluent and draw on their lexical store.

7. Using texts

As noted above, if learners are to develop an interlanguage where the lexical combinations are not merely grammatical but appropriately natural, meaning that they are "in tune" with other speakers, they must be exposed to authentic texts, both oral and written – and plenty of them.

As well as having a language focus, taking a task-based approach is normally thought of in the context of speaking skills, but there is no reason why it should not be extended to the other skills, so that working with texts will not simply be the stimulus for the main task, but part of the task itself.

While encouraging extensive reading is beyond the scope of this book, we have for several of our tasks here provided ideas for how texts might be central to task performance. Students should be allowed time to respond to the stimulus text, where there is one, in the lead in. This may involve a more extensive pre-task stage, such as for the task called **5b Talking about a song**, in which there is a sample text learners can "mine" text for written language in preparation for the coming task (Willis and Willis 2007: 133). One way to do this is to set reading these texts as homework.

Later in the lesson sequence, texts can move centre-stage as the basis for a discussion, for example for **3f FutureTech** to set the scene for a problem or puzzle to be solved; or as "jigsaws" to provide an information gap (**4a Bad neighbours**); to stimulate questions; or in mini-research projects.

Even in a task that focuses on speaking, learners will have the chance to read or listen to a model of the task being completed. We have provided more samples here on the downloadable audio recordings, but you can consider how you might adapt these to make them suitable for their learners in terms of level, needs and interests.

8. The value of task repetition

"Repetition serves to reduce the processing load, facilitate conversational development, and also makes things less threatening." (Skehan 1998: 34)

"when procedural knowledge is 'automatized' or fine-tuned, it is implicit" Klapper (2003), in Mike Long, **In Defense of Tasks and TBLT (2016)**

Those who, like Zoltan Dörnyei (2015), support a **skill-building theory** of language based on the work of DeKeyser and others, believe that explicit knowledge can be converted into implicit knowledge through **proceduralisation.** (Long's view differs from this in that he claims that intentional learning and explicit knowledge only *aid the development* of implicit knowledge, rather than undergoing some kind of conversion.).

This is for all intents and purposes what teachers understand by the more familiar term controlled – or restricted – practice, except that it is now supported by a more sophisticated cognitive model of language learning. In task-based learning, one way to achieve this kind of practice is by **task repetition**; more suggestions for practice with an explicit language focus follow in the second section, **Micro-strategies**.

Task repetition means inevitably recycling lexis. Having to retrieve high-frequency words and hearing the words from a classmate and having to retrieve their meanings are equally useful. To learn an item of vocabulary, it may be necessary to encounter a word more than ten times (Nation, I.S.P. (2013). Reading outside class is perhaps the most important factor involved here, but repeating tasks also contributes to this process, and this is a reason to build not only immediate repetition, but **distributed practice** into a learning programme.

Repetitive tasks help to develop students' fluency, and this is one of the "four strands" that Paul Nation considers should, in equal balance, constitute effective language programmes (Nation, 2010). In Nation's conception, activities which build fluency are simply those which provide learners with opportunities to work with already familiar language in relatively undemanding ways. The least demanding of all is to repeat the task with no variations – though usually with the students' groups recombined.

In addition, when a task is repeated in this way, it may enable learners to add linguistic complexity, perhaps assisted by a teacher-led feedback and clarification stage (See **FonF**, above.) Research has shown that repeating a familiar task seems to engage learners in more **syntactic processing:** they are able to focus more on grammatical accuracy, for one thing; and they appear to be able to use lexis more precisely, including organising lexis. (Bygate, in Willis & Willis eds, 1996). For all these reasons, repetition appears in traditional models of the task cycle.

9. Conclusion: the main advantages of task-based learning

Here is a short list of advantages of adopting a more task-based approach:

- It is an approach that acknowledges that language is not just a menu of structures to be learned and practised; it a way of **understanding and expressing *meanings***. Meaning is central to the tasks in this book.

- It is a way of learning language that **involves the whole person**, so it is likely to appeal to all types of learners – those who have a more socially-orientated holistic view, as well as those who are more analytically inclined.

- It is an **evidence-based approach**; it is well supported by theories of how languages are learned, even though these processes are as yet incompletely understood.

- In the pre-task stages, and at other stages, it allows learners to be exposed to **a rich diet of authentic language** rather than a pre-selected and rather limited menu of structures devised by an author or publisher.

- It is likely to be **enjoyable.** Students will enjoy the variety of contexts in which they can try out language; teachers can be flexible in when and how they focus on the formal features of emergent language.

1 Micro-strategies and tools

This section aims to support teachers looking for more practical guidance with implementing a task-based approach.

1. Pre-task micro-strategies

a) Preparation and thinking time

The **length and complexity of a given task can vary considerably** – from a simple, informal one-minute discussion (e.g. *who had the best weekend and why?*) to a more structured long -term project (e.g. agreeing on and producing the content for a class magazine). The more complex a task, relative to learner level and the familiarity of the topic, the greater the need to **scaffold** the activity i.e. offer the support learners need to complete the task successfully. This can be online, while the task is occurring, as and when learners need it, through your monitoring (see **section 2**). Ideally, though, support occurs through preparing learners sufficiently for the task before they begin. This is why you will see in our tasks plenty of pre-task preparation stages. What happens here varies, but generally, a pre-task phase consists of some or all of the following elements, so keep them in mind if you are designing your own tasks or would like to adapt the ones we suggest in the book:

Pre-task activity	Purpose / rationale	Sample procedures
The topic of the task is established and discussed	To build interest; **to activate schema**; to ready learners for the task	Discussion of the general topic through a prompt or visuals, personalised discussion, or through a text e.g. a teacher anecdote
Students prepare their ideas for the task	To allow students time/space to focus on what the task requires in terms of content, thereby improving the quality of their contributions during the task	Students complete a worksheet with prompts related to the task; students take notes regarding what they want to say; students brainstorm based on relevant prompts
Key language for the task is pre-taught	To facilitate successful completion of the task*	Matching lexis to definitions/visuals; feeding in/eliciting and boarding useful items; listening to student ideas and upgrading them; brainstorming topic/task lexis
Task parameters are made clear: 1) specific parameters of the task 2) the goal of the task 3) interaction pattern and roles 4) time limit 5) what and how students are expected to report in post-task feedback	To ensure students are able to proceed through the task independently, working towards the goal, and are ready to report back on the task	Through verbal instructions; through teacher-fronted demonstration; through demonstration involving the students; using the board/IWB to flag up elements of the task

* When providing input/focusing on language *prior* to a task, it is very important to:

- keep this limited: overwhelming the learners with new language will take up valuable cognitive space and sideline the task itself;
- keep it brief: the main event of the lesson is the task itself, not the language provided in support of it;
- be clear: the language is there to help the students with the task and is *not* the primary aim of the activity (many students are habituated to assume production following language input is there for them to *display* their abilities with the new language – this is true of PPP but not TBL).

b) Establishing task goals

As we mentioned in the introduction, a task should be purposeful: students should be communicating with each other, with a need to both speak and listen. This is why **a task goal or outcome plays a key role in the task phase**. We have suggested goals/outcomes in our sample tasks in subsequent sections. However, we would encourage teachers to supplement and adapt coursebook material and standard skills activities to make them more meaning-oriented, and task-like. One strategy for doing so is to add an explicit goal/outcome to an activity when giving instructions to learners. Here are some possible goals/outcomes which could work for a range of activities – select as suits the given activity:

> *"(Tasks) are goal-oriented. In other words, the emphasis is on understanding and conveying meanings in order to complete the task successfully. While learners are doing tasks, they are using the language in a meaningful way."*
>
> Willis (1996)

- **Speak, listen and evaluate:** A communicates, B listens in order to offer their own opinion concerning what they have heard. Example: *Listen to your partner's ideas for spending the money and then say what you agree or disagree with.*
- **Speak, listen and enquire:** A communicates, B listens and either during or after asks follow-up questions for more information. Example: *Listen to your partner's nostalgia story and think of at least three more things you would like to know.*
- **Speak, listen and solve:** A and B offer their views based on the stimulus and work to solve a problem/reach consensus as part of the task. Example: *Share your ideas for improving your neighbourhood, and then agree on the best three.*
- **Speak, listen and identify:** A and B communicate in order to find similarities/differences in response to the stimulus; or to identify which information they are hearing is true and which is false. *Listen to your partner's summary of the article. Can you find any differences from the information in yours?*
- **Speak, listen and report:** A and B take turns, speaking and listening, with a view to reporting back key points they heard to the class or to a new partner. *Take turns to tell each other about your story. Listen carefully, because you will later tell a new partner what you heard.*
- **Speak, listen and vote:** students prepare a presentation. They present it to other students, as well as listening to each other pair's presentation. At the end, they decide which other presentation was the best/most interesting/persuasive etc. *Give your presentation for your product – be confident and persuade the listener! When you have listened to the other presentations, choose the one you think is most convincing.*

Not all real-life communication involves an explicit goal – we spend a lot of time simply sharing experiences and views, for instance. We have found that it is best to select a goal/outcome for a task that feels most natural and organic to the act of communication that is occurring; for example, if students are sharing experiences, a goal/outcome that encourages them to react and ask follow-up questions feels more authentic.

2. On-task micro-strategies

Facilitating the task

The aim of pre-task work is to encourage students to communicate with each other independently, with minimal interventions from the teacher during the task itself. The role of the teacher during the task, then, is to **be attentive but more or less invisible** – monitoring should be remote in the sense that students are hardly aware of the teacher's presence while they are engaged with the task. This does not mean the teacher should switch off, tempting though it may be! The following are effective strategies for the teacher to implement while the students are on task:

Listen, observe, note
Let the students begin; circulate and monitor, checking students are on-task – this is the most important initial role, as it is difficult, especially with larger classes, to be sure all students have fully grasped instructions. Consider doing the following: • move immediately to pairs/groups who you feel may not have grasped all instructions (perhaps they were further away from you while the task was set up, or are not as strong in their level or listening skills…or you have noticed that today they seem tired or distracted!); • circulate, pausing briefly by each pair/group and listening to check they are on task; • circulate again, spending more time with each pair/group, listening but not intervening, but instead taking notes to inform the post-task phases (see **Task feedback** and **Feedback templates**).

Intervene where necessary
We suggest the teacher is largely invisible, but this should not be at the expense of not being available when it serves the students and the task. You may do the following: • gently and supportively prompt students who do not seem to be fully on task. This is why it is useful, with more complex tasks, to bullet the components of the task on the board/IWB so you can refer students to them. Remind them of what they should do, give examples and steer them so they move back on track; • provide students with a phrase or sentence when it helps them move on with the task (following the principle of **recasts** mentioned earlier); • remind the whole class of the time limit if you feel it is useful to do so, warning them they have, say, 2 or 3 minutes left. **Don't feel you need to stick to a time limit you initially gave** – if students are engaged and on-task, feel pleased and be flexible in allowing it to run for longer than planned. Do, though, be aware of the value of post-task stages, so leave plenty of time for these; • keep early finishers occupied. It is very rare for all students to complete a task at the same time, so it is worth being prepared to offer something to those who finish before others. Check they have completed all elements of the task; extend the task – for example, ask them to agree on one more solution; let them know you will call on them first to present ideas on feedback, so they should spend the remaining time readying this; ask them if there were any items of language they needed while doing the task that you can help them; or, if you happened to note any language issues they had when previously circulating, offer these now (see **Feedback slips**).

Effective monitoring is key in a student-centred, communicative classroom – it is also one of the most difficult roles of a teacher to get right (i.e. to monitor usefully and meaningfully, balancing attentiveness and remoteness). Experiment and reflect on monitoring strategies that seemed to work for you and the students. Overall, try to remain present for the duration of the task, while not feeling guilty if you need to catch your breath every now and then.

3. Post-task micro-strategies

a) Task feedback: content feedback

As tasks are goal-focused, the immediate priority in post-task feedback is to have the students report on the task goal and process: whether they successfully completed the task, presenting reports, or sharing interesting experiences / views they hear, or even problems that occurred in resolving the task. This can be called **content feedback**. Content feedback will often take care of itself – if the goal was clear, and students were motivated, discussion in feedback should flow freely. It pays, however, to adopt strategies to ensure effective content feedback. Consider implementing the following:

- double check before the task occurs that all students are clear on the outcome and aware they will report back on this in front of their peers;
- while adopting the **listen, observe, note** monitoring strategy above, identify opinions and exchanges that are worth sharing in content feedback – this could be a particularly interesting, unusual or controversial view, for example. Nominate the relevant students, asking them to share this (for example: *Andras, I was really interested in what you said to Sara about bad summer holidays – can you share this with the rest of the class?*);
- use the **Feedback templates** in tools to take notes not just for language feedback but also content feedback, if it helps you remember who to nominate to contribute to content feedback;
- elicit **process feedback** – ask students to reflect on the task: what they enjoyed, what was challenging, whether they feel satisfied they communicated clearly and accurately; this can help provide a segue to the focus on language.

b) Task feedback: focus on form 1 – incidental and emergent language

We believe it is valid to offer **recasts** to students during the actual task (see the introduction for more on the value of recasts). Given the fact that students are expected to complete tasks independently, it follows that most of the **work done on language will occur *after* the main task phase.** This is a major point of principle and procedure that sets TBL apart from more accuracy-focused paradigms such as PPP.

Dealing with language that emerges can be challenging – by definition, one has planned how to do this less. One key strategy is to anticipate the areas of language that may emerge naturally as part of the process of completing the task. This is why in the task descriptions in the main section of the book we have offered suggestions for areas that seem likely to be inherent to the task, or useful in moving towards completing the task goal (see the **Language feedback options** summary that accompanies each task).

> *"Language is so vast and varied that we can never provide learners with a viable and comprehensive description of the language as a whole. We can, however, provide them with guidelines and, more important, we can provide them with activities which encourage them to think about samples of language and to draw their own conclusions about how language works."*
>
> Willis and Willis, 1996

"Tuning in" to areas of linguistic need readies you as a teacher to deal with them if they do occur. Quite aside from this, the communication-rich environment of a task-based lesson will provide many **affordances** – chances for students to attend to, and begin to acquire, language that emerges as salient to the student in the context of the task. We cannot fully predict these, but we can prepare and implement strategies to help us identify, capture and exploit – **ICE** – this incidental emergent language.

- **I: *identify*** – listen and notice language that is inaccurate or unnatural (the latter is important – aim to go beyond identifying slips that can easily be self-corrected: look to where students could use more sophisticated language e.g. more natural collocations).

- **C: *capture*** – have a clear system for noting language you feel the students could work on after the task. See **Feedback templates** and **Feedback slips**.
- **E: *exploit*** – having identified language – whether lexis or grammatical structures – that emerged from the task, clarify and practice this language. See **Instant Practice Ideas** in tools below.

c) Task feedback: focus on form 2 – structured consciousness-raising through text-mining

As well as capturing and working with emergent language, many tasks involve the use of texts at some point in the cycle. These can be returned to and "mined" for language in the post-task focus on form phase. As we have noted, in TBL, we are generally not concerned with presenting and practising a single item of language; it adopts a more holistic approach to language focus. The Willis quotation on the previous page defines how we can draw attention to a range of linguistic items, through what is known as **consciousness-raising (C-R)** i.e. drawing attention to items and patterns that students may otherwise miss, and through repeated practice of this, developing the student's ability to do it more autonomously both inside and outside the classroom. You can find example consciousness-raising templates in the Additional resources **section**. A related term, already mentioned in the introduction, is **noticing** – where students are encouraged to attend to specific language and identify gaps between their own output and that of a proficient speaker (see **7 Whole class tasks** for more information on how to facilitate noticing).

We want students to get to the point where they can autonomously identify language of interest in a text. This requires sensitising and training, however. When asking students to look at language in a text, scaffold the process by selecting from a range of C-R activities/question types, using a variety of the examples below to help students notice lexical patterns, grammatical structures and discourse markers or other cohesive devices:

This table is based in part on Willis and Willis (1996), as well as Willis (1996).

Identifying – students are guided to pick out particular lexical or grammatical items of interest:
• There are four examples of *make* in the text and three examples of *do* – find them and underline the nouns they collocate with.   • Find examples of the modal *would* in the text. Sometimes it is contracted!   • Look for four different ways parts of sentences are joined together (apart from *and*).   • Find examples of *have*. When is it connected to possession, and when is it not?   • In paragraph 1, there is the expression *black and white*. Find three more X and Y expressions.   • Find three phrases with *of* (in the second half of the text).   • How many examples of *it* can you find in the final paragraph? What does each refer to?

Classifying – students find and/or categorise lexical/structural items according to semantic or formal properties:
• Find and underline the adjectives used to describe his feelings about the holiday. Which are positive and which are negative? What prepositions follow some of the adjectives?   • Underline verbs that relate to the past in the second paragraph. Which are about single actions and which are repeated actions?   • There are four idioms about money – find them and decide if they relate to having enough money, not enough money, too much money.   • Look for eight words ending in *–ed/-ing*. Are these adjectives or verbs?

Hypothesis checking – here, students are given a rule/feature of language and asked to match it to instances in the text:

- *Would* can be used for imaginary situations and to talk about past habits. In the text, which use is more common? Can you find an example of each?
- The present perfect can be used to talk about finished actions in the past, and actions that are still true. Find examples of either in the text.
- *Anyway* can be used by a speaker to start talking again, as well as to show they are ready to finish. Which use can you see in the transcript?

d) Task repetition

What we have written so far suggests that a task is completed once, and then forgotten. This would be a shame, to say the least. Effective syllabus design often employs a **spiral** approach to sequencing – the same language area is revisited later, usually in a different way that adds variety and complexity to what has previously been studied promoting longer term retention of the specific language area. The same is true for TBL: there is evidence that repeating a task leads to improved performance in the task, and possible gains to knowledge of and ability to use aspects of the language system (see Bygate, in Willis and Willis, 1996) (but with TBL, potentially a *variety* of language areas, as we are not concerned with limiting ourselves to a single language area).

Tasks can be repeated within the same lesson, or in subsequent lessons, as suits the constraints of the particular lesson or broader syllabus. It may be repeated once, or many times, depending on the scale of the task, and learner motivation. The latter point hints at the criticism that is levelled at task repetition – isn't repetition boring? It can be, but this can be mitigated or circumvented entirely not just by selecting tasks that appeal to your learners but also by implementing variables related to task performance. If you repeat a task, then, consider implementing one or more of following variables that help you tweak the task to keep it fresh and to keep students motivated to engage with the task outcome:

- New partners/new interaction (e.g. pairs to groups; new physical format*);
- new task goal/outcome (see **Task goals/outcomes** above for ideas);
- Task content varied (e.g. change topic while keeping the task similar in format; change parameters such as how many points learners need to agree on);
- Task made more demanding (e.g. don't allow learners to consult notes; reduce the time available for completing the task).

*The format you use for a task should be based on what appears to be most suitable for the task. Some options for both initial task and repeated task include:

- **Pairs:** two students work together.
- **Groups:** three or more students work together.
- **Mingle:** students walk around freely talking to a range of people.
- **Ladder:** students line up facing each other and communicate with the person opposite. Every now and then, the teacher gives a signal and *one* line moves down one person, giving everyone a new partner.
- **Carousel/Onion circles:** the same as a ladder, except students are arranged in two concentric circles rather than lines.
- **Buzz groups:** students walk around the room, moving between stations at which they are required to do something (e.g. discuss a series of prompts, or comment on a visual).

4. Tools

The tools outlined below are designed to facilitate **ICE** above – identifying, capturing and exploiting incidental and emerging language.

1. Feedback templates

As mentioned earlier, while students are on task, it is important to be purposefully engaged with listening to their output, in order to identify and capture language worth focusing on. You might decide to put this straight on the board, while monitoring, or type it in, in the case of an IWB. Or you might take notes as you go along, with a view to selecting the most useful and interesting for post-task language feedback. We find it helps enormously if you have a template to use for this. What form this takes is up to you, but here are some suggestions (imagine these as A4 sized, to be used as you monitor, and then selected from after the task is finished):

a) Good / bad

Successful language	Errors

This is useful as it reminds us that we can share instances of excellent language use, affording us opportunities for peer teaching.

b) Grammar / lexis / pronunciation

Grammar	Lexis	Pronunciation

It is easy to overlook issues with sounds, stress and intonation; this reminds us that pronunciation is integral to clearly and accurately expressing what we mean.

c) Individual feedback 1 (whole class)

Student	Good example	Error
Andras		
Tibor		
Sara		
Judit		
Ali		
Jin		
Erika		
Lubomir		
Olga		

This encourages us to spread our attention across a range of students, rather than staying focused on the most vocal, stronger or weaker (or the ones we can hear more easily!). It allows us to publicly share good examples of language, boosting confidence. You will need to decide whether the errors should remain anonymous – there is good reason *not* to keep an error anonymous (knowing the error is relevant to you means you are more likely to attend to it), but also good reason not to flag up an error an individual has made in a public way (it can be embarrassing). Decide based on how well the students know each other, cultural attitudes to error correction, and mood.

d) Individual feedback 2 (single learner log)

Andras	What you said	What you should say
1.		
2.		
3.		
4.		
5.		

This involves keeping a log for each student and noting issues over the course of a lesson or several lessons. This is then given to the student to work on – they can collaborate in groups to improve the sentence in the second column, writing a correction in the third column. When this is completed, the teacher checks it. This solves the problem of public correction: it can be done more safely individually, though we prefer it as a pair or small group activity. Clearly, it is harder to implement on a practical level, especially with larger classes, but students tend to be very appreciative of the individual attention it provides.

2. Feedback slips

Instead of having A4 paper or typing the error into your pc/tablet, bring in a number of slips of paper (ideally, the blank side of scrap paper). Each slip should be big enough to write a sentence on. As you monitor, identify and capture what the student said, noting their name on it too. At the language focus stage, distribute slips to the relevant students. There are two options:

- The slip contains the error and a recast of what the students said:

- The slip contains the error, which students now work on, trying to correct it:

An alternative is to keep the slips anonymous; put them in the middle of the room, and have pairs come to examine one at a time, deciding if it is correct or incorrect, and correcting the latter. The corrections are checked in feedback and useful language boarded.

Note that feedback slips are also a good strategy for keeping "early finishers" occupied – if a pair finishes the task a few minutes before others, then ask them to look through the slips. In the subsequent language focus stage with the rest of the class, they can function as "experts"/teaching assistants, helping guide the other pairs.

3. Whiteboard/IWB

When dealing with emerging language, a clear centralised record of what has come up is hugely important. At the end of focus on form, new structures and lexis should be clearly presented on the board. The layout of the board can be similar to one of the templates above, or could look something like this:

Sentences for correction	New phrases
I was only late 15 minutes.	a flying visit
Our connection was more informal.	oversleep vs. sleep in
She didn't let me to go to the party.	be responsible for "it's not my responsibility"
He's not people person.	
If I would have done it sooner, there wouldn't been problems.	take time "it takes me ……to…"
It's something what I use every day for working.	(15 minutes/a long time)
I had so good time in the end.	It was tasty. It tasted (really) good.
I became nervous for the traffic.	I'm not (really) a fan of…

On the left there are full sentences that have emerged, with some form of error: this can become an activity/game by which students in groups attempt to correct the sentences. It's very important that the final record shows *correct* sentences and that students know not to note down the defective ones.

On the right are words, phrases and collocations that have come up during the lesson. These, along with the sentences on the left, once corrected, can now be exploited for spontaneous instant practice.

4. Instant practice ideas

Instant practice allows you to put the words and items to work, to exploit them in the remaining time left in the lesson. It is not easy to spontaneously devise language practice activities, though! We advise you have a toolkit of activity types you can use as and when needed to practice what has come up in a meaningful, engaging way.

a) Progressive deletion (Willis, 1996)

- Number the items on the board. Call out the numbers and have the students say the item out loud. Once you have done this for all items, do it again, randomly, but this time, delete elements of the item (e.g. part of the sentence, or half of a collocation, or letters from a word) and continue this, making it increasingly difficult by erasing more elements; students are forced to employ their powers of recall.

b) Personalised use

- Students ask each other questions using the items on the board/in their notebooks.
- As above but extended – use a template such as the one below to create a questionnaire using the items. Students then mingle and survey each other, writing in names and key words into the final column for feedback.

	Question	Who answered/what they said
1.		
2.		
3.		
4.		
5.		

- Students write a number of true/false sentences about their life using the items; they then play a game in pairs or groups to guess which are true and which are false.
- **2d Me not me** – use the format of the task as a way to practice new language. Students place new items on a cline, depending on to what extent they associate the item with their life/feelings or not.

c) Error correction

- Erase the board and ask students to close their notebooks. Dictate a number of sentences using the items but getting an element of form or meaning wrong e.g. *I'm afraid from high place.*
- Students write down the sentences and then in pairs/groups correct them.
- As above but make it a competition, with pairs "wagering" money on each sentence depending on how confident they are. Give each pair a certain amount of money to start with e.g. £100.

d) Grammaticisation

- Remove sentences from the board. Dictate (or board) key words from those sentences and then ask the students to reconstruct the sentences as accurately as possible. So, for example, the sentence on the board was: *Bob used to go to the gym all the time*; *Bob/used/gym/time* is boarded or dictated.

5. Capturing and preserving – longer term access and retention

A final point: emergent language is not there, on paper, in a coursebook – it feels more ephemeral and we need to ensure there is a centralised record which the students and teacher can use to review and return to the language. So think about how the language will not just be captured but "preserved" for future reference. Here are some brief suggestions:

- Have the students take photos of the board.
- Print out/send the final board record to all students, in the case of IWBs.
- Keep a log of either of the above.
- Use an app such as *Quizlet*: you, or the students, can input lexical items or sentences, and their meaning (or visuals, opposites etc), and then plan a variety of games in your own time or in class-time.
- Encourage and train students to keep logical records in a vocabulary notebook.

5. Designing your own tasks

a) Types of task in this book

Most of the rest of this book is devoted to sample tasks. These have roughly been grouped according to Willis's taxonomy of tasks. Some of the tasks could easily have been placed in another section – and some task sequences contain several types of task. It is better to think of the grouping as approximate rather than watertight:

- **Categorising:** tasks which involve the students working to list, rank, group or sort based on some criteria. For instance, in **2b Domestic robot** learners follow a pyramid format to rank domestic chores they would have an AI servant perform for them.
- **Opinion gaps:** tasks where students compare views and experiences on a given subject, finding out how much (or how little) they have in common. An example is **3f FutureTech** where learners read descriptions of potential technological innovations, and share views on how likely each one is, as well as how useful or dangerous.
- **Problem-solving:** with these, learners engage with a stimulus to solve a particular problem or mystery. The format can vary – for instance, in **4a Bad neighbours**, learners engage with a jigsaw listening to hear "two sides of the story" with neighbours who do not get on, in order to arbitrate and take action; in **4d Identity swap** learners assume the identity of their partner, answering questions as they anticipate the partner would, before reflecting on how accurately they assumed the identity.
- **Sharing personal experiences**: these are tasks where learners simply share and explore something personal to them, whether childhood memories (**5a Nostalgia story**), music that is important to them (**5b Talking about a song**) or sharing homespun remedies to illnesses passed down the family (**5g Folk remedies**).
- **Creative tasks:** here students use their imagination as much as their own personal experiences; whether to create the details of a movie based upon its score (**6c Soundtracks**) or through drawing a "masterpiece" which is then evaluated in a gallery format, before they pitch their own work in order to sell it (**6e The struggling artist**).
- **Text reconstruction:** this is our own addition to the Willis taxonomy. In these tasks, learners collaborate to reconstruct a typically short text from its key words, before examining differences between their version and the original. The most well-known of this type of task is **7a Dictogloss**.

Our hope is that you find something useful for your learners in these tasks. However, we really hope they inspire you to adapt them and create your *own* tasks – ones that are more suitable for your particular students.

b) A checklist for designing your own tasks

We have devised a checklist to facilitate the process of you designing your own tasks. When it comes to adapting or designing a task, ask yourself the following questions:

Selecting task content, format and goal

- What will the precise content of the task be and is this motivating for my students…will they happily engage with this, find it useful and stimulating?
- What type of task is it, with reference to the types above? How is the need to communicate and collaborate created?
- Related to this, what is the goal of the main task?

Pre-task: creating the right conditions

- How will you introduce the task and generate interest in it?
- What scaffolding do the students need to maximise task performance – thinking time, preparation time, note-taking, pre-teaching of key lexis?

On task: letting the students work independently

- Has the goal been made explicit to all students?
- What format/interaction will the task take (e.g. groups, pairs, mingle) and has this been made clear?
- Am I ready to *listen, observe and note* in a non-intrusive way? Do I have a system for capturing interesting content for the content feedback, and possible language for the post-task language focus?

Post-task 1: content feedback

- How will students report and share their route to the goal with each other?
- Is this simply discussion/comparison, or is there a product to be shared?
- Can I use my notes – what I heard – to facilitate this?

Post-task 2: focus on language

- How does the focus on language come about?
  A: through emergent language that I have captured;
  B: through a teacher model that I now provide of the task;
  C: through exposing students to a written or oral text related to the task;
  D: through a combination of the above?
- Will this focus be a particular language point that is useful for the students, or through noticing/consciousness-raising of a variety of forms?
- Do I feel able to provide immediate practice of this language point?

Task repetition

- Is it appropriate to repeat the task immediately, in the same lesson, or later?
- How will I vary the task repetition, in terms of goal, format, interaction?
- Have I built in time/space for students to incorporate new language, language that is useful for them in terms of improving task performance?

2 Categorising

2a Crime and punishment

 About the activity

Task type	ranking
Task outcome	Students rank crimes according to their seriousness, and then co-operate to decide on the appropriate sentence for each.

Introduction

Crime is never far from the headlines and it features in many course book units. It's a good subject for discussion, and can be approached by using a real-life example of a surprising judicial decision. This is a controversial topic and so may need to be handled carefully, especially in the light of any recent news stories.

Variation, extension, task repetition

- Students can create their own ideas based on crimes they have heard about, and share these as a class – for a second run of the main task.

- Students can read more about one of the cases below. The case of Ronald Stanford, the teenage boy who was sentenced to 170 years in prison, works well. Because of the circumstances of this case, it is one that leads to plenty of discussion.

- Role-play. For this, you need two copies of each scenario. Each pair takes one idea and plans with her partner (the defence counsel) the reasons why she is innocent. Obviously, there needs to be adequate preparation time for this – around 10 minutes. Each pair should also prepare some questions to ask another pair in role as prosecution lawyers. In the final part of the role-play, everyone listens, the class (the jury) decides if the defendant is innocent or guilty and one student (the judge) decides on the appropriate sentence.

Language feedback options

- Modal verbs + perfect infinitive, especially *should/shouldn't have*; hypotheticals e.g. *That would encourage other people to…* Passives: *was sentenced to X years in prison, made to, the sentence was reduced*
- Lexis: *responsible for, guilty of*
- Legal language such as *a verdict, sentence, fine of X, special (extenuating) circumstances, got off lightly, harsh/lenient punishment, plead/find someone innocent or guilty, got away with it, under curfew, tag (noun, verb), false allegation, diminished responsibility*
- Language for opinions and comparison *I think that's too harsh/lenient, I think he should be made to + V; I don't think he deserves to + V*

How to run the activity

Levels	B1+
Ages	teens, young adult
Length	30–40 minutes

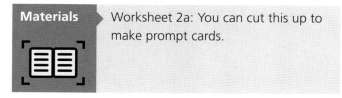

Materials — Worksheet 2a: You can cut this up to make prompt cards.

Pre-task

To set the theme at the start of the lesson, choose a recent example of a court case from the news. Students can then discuss what, in their opinion, would have been an appropriate sentence. Afterwards you can tell them what actually happened. Here is an example text:

> *A reclusive farmer who lives alone with his three dogs in a remote village is woken by the sound of intruders in his house. These turn out to be two teenage burglars. The farmer shoots them with a shotgun – one is killed and the other is injured. What do you think the correct sentence should be? (Did he fire the gun in anger? Remember he was trying to defend his property.)*
>
> *In the end, the farmer was sentenced to a minimum of 9 years in prison for murder; this sentence was later reduced to 5 years for manslaughter.*

Task 1 (optional)

The task may follow a course book unit dealing with crimes and criminals. Otherwise you will need to brainstorm crimes with students or show them a pre-prepared list. These should be pre-taught, especially to lower levels. A more student-centred way of doing this is having students match the crimes to definitions.

- In pairs, students rank the crimes from most to least serious – for example, they may sort them first into violent and non-violent crimes.
- The task is now to think of what an appropriate punishment would be for each crime. (You will also need to help the students with language such as *pay a fine* and *community service*.) At the start of this stage, you may want to get students to listen to two people discussing their opinions of suitable punishments for two of the crimes.
- Early finishers can consider which factors would aggravate or mitigate the crime, for example, the fact that the farmer was trying to defend his property.

The main task

- Use the worksheet. You can fold it or cut it into situation cards.
- In groups, students discuss the real-life cases one by one and decide what sentence they would hand down. It is important that they agree on what the sentence should be.
- Afterwards, the groups appoint a spokesperson who should tell the class what the decision of the group is. Take the opportunity to discuss differences of opinion which arise.
- Finally, compare the sentences with the actual sentences of the court, provided on the right.

Fold the paper.

Read about the crimes and decide what you think the correct prison sentence should be.

Compare your decisions with the actual sentences which were handed down.

The crime	The punishment
A teenage mother who works as a cashier in a shop allows her friends to shoplift goods, and turns a blind eye.	The mother (and her baby) was sentenced to jail for six months, but the friends were allowed to go free.
A great grandmother sells a goldfish to a 14-year old boy. (It is illegal to sell pets to children.)	The grandmother was fined £1000, put under curfew and fitted with an electronic tag.
A man repeatedly steals women's underwear from houses and washing lines. He has done it 120 times.	The man was sent to jail for two and a half years.
Five men use a stolen tractor, break into a factory and steal £20,000 worth of "jammie dodgers" (a type of biscuit) – about 240,000 biscuits in all.	The gang leader was sent to prison for 44 months, and the others for between 60 and 40 months. (The one who pleaded guilty got 40 months.)
A 15-year old and 13-year old commit a double murder of two elderly women as part of an attempted robbery; the younger boy stole $5. On the evidence of his friend, he is convicted for both murders.	One boy got a 5-year sentence – and was released after 2 years and 2 days. The younger boy was sentenced to 170 years in prison.
A teenager finds that a large sum of money has been deposited by accident in his bank account. By the time the bank finds out, he has spent $30,000 on a BMW.	The teenager was sentenced to 10 years in prison.
Someone with 56,000 followers on Twitter hints in a tweet that a public figure has committed a very serious crime.	The person who tweeted had to pay £15,000 *in damages to* the victim.

ACTIVITIES FOR TASK-BASED LEARNING
by Neil Anderson and Neil McCutcheon

© DELTA Publishing, 2019 | www.deltapublishing.co.uk
ISBN 978-3-12-501701-6

2b Domestic robot

 About the activity

Task type	pyramid discussion
Task outcome	Students co-operate in groups to prioritise which "apps" they would like installed on a domestic robot.

Introduction

Artificial Intelligence (AI) has increasingly entered public discourse in terms of algorithms and "bots" that work behind the scenes to enhance our web browsing experience, and even spy on us. To what extent jobs will become automated can be a lively topic of discussion.

This task takes a lighter look at AI, together with pet peeve chores. The format is that of a pyramid discussion. We first heard of this classic task type in **Keep Talking** by Friederike Klippel (1984). We heard of a robot version via a blogpost about a presentation by Jeremy Harmer.

Variation, extension, task repetition

Creating your own pyramid discussions

The principle of these discussions is that students have to narrow their choices and prioritise, reaching agreement in co-operation in pairs and groups. Obviously, the flexibility of groupings is determined by the number of students in a class. You need to decide in advance what these will be. Individual work > pairs > two groups of four is ideal, but classes in multiples of 16 are rare. Here are some topics that work well in this format:

- You are in a shipwreck off the shore of a desert island. You will be there for a year. You have to decide on a list of items to rescue and take with you. (You can limit these by specifying that they must be portable, and you might want to say that the satellite phone is broken!)
- A playlist of the best songs that reflect your era, or which people/events to include in a yearbook.
- Nominations for the best band/game/sportsperson/book of all time.

Language feedback options

- Typically, this task includes comparatives and superlatives when describing the chores: "Doing the dishes is *more tedious* than weeding the garden." And modal language e.g. "But you *don't have to* go outside!"
- You can sequence words on a cline to describe preferences: *can't stand – don't mind – love + ing.*
- Other language that arises is to do with managing the interactions and the task itself: *It's your turn… What do you think? … I prefer X's suggestion…, include, delete, put in, leave out*

▶ How to run the activity

Levels	A2–B2
Ages	teens, young adult
Length	30–40 minutes*

Materials	Worksheet 2b: The worksheet is intended to give structure to the discussion. You may prefer not to use a worksheet.

*The task can be run with or without tight time limits.
 At each stage you can decide what you think will work best.

Pre-task

- Get students talking about household chores. The vocabulary is essential and may have to be pre-taught with lower levels. This could be done with initial brainstorming, or by showing the students pictures of various chores and finding out which ones they know the names of in English.
- Record any of these that are unfamiliar on the whiteboard.

Task

- Instruct task. Set the scene with a preamble e.g. *the government is keen to take some popular measures and so they have decided to issue each household with a domestic robot to carry out certain chores.* Show a picture of a robot.
- Individually, the students use the worksheet to write down in any order which ten "apps" they would like installed into the robot e.g. it should be able to do the ironing. They have two minutes to decide. Tell them they will only get the apps they are able to write down in that time.
- When the two minutes are up, students stop writing. Tell them that the government has had to make cutbacks and therefore the robot has to be shared with the next-door neighbour. Furthermore, it will only come loaded with six apps. In pairs, students choose which they would like most.
- Stop the discussions. It's important to have no feedback at this stage. Repeat the part about cutbacks. It turns out that now the robot will have to be shared with everyone on your floor (in your block) and that students will only have five apps between them. Once again, they will only get the apps they agree on.
- It's possible to have another stage in still larger groups, and forcing a shorter list of options. If you do this, groups will need to appoint a chairperson.
- Depending on the size of your class, you will probably want to move on to the plenary stage now. In preparation, the groups should choose a spokesperson who will report back to the whole class. The group co-operates to help this person plan by writing down the reasons for their five choices.
- Each group reports back to the class, and if you like you can record the choices on the whiteboard for a final vote on the three top priorities.

2b Domestic robot

The government has decided to issue each household with one prototype robotic assistant, pre-programmed to do 10 of your least favourite chores (within and beyond the confines of your house/flat). Which 10 apps would you install? e.g. ironing. And why?

1	
2	
3	
4	
5	
6	
7	
8	
9	
10	

Now await further instructions…

 © DELTA Publishing, 2019 | www.deltapublishing.co.uk
ISBN 978-3-12-501701-6

ACTIVITIES FOR TASK-BASED LEARNING
by Neil Anderson and Neil McCutcheon

2c Dangerous animals

 About the activity

Task type	Listing/ranking
Task outcome	Students itemise dangerous animals, and then decide on how dangerous they seem in relation to each other.

Introduction

This listing and ranking task works particularly well with younger learners – however, if you feel it is appropriate for an adult group, go ahead! The task balances output and input. Students have to do a lot of speaking and negotiation as they agree on their lists; but later, when they check their assumptions regarding dangerous animals against the Fact File in Worksheet 2, there are plenty of opportunities to notice and work with relevant language items related to the topic.

Variation, extension, task repetition

- With lower level students, you may want to pre-teach some of the core vocabulary so they can evaluate how dangerous each animal is (see the first point in language focus).
- If you have less time, or are worried about potential difficulty in the texts, reduce the number of animals from nine to six.
- Jigsaw: you can give students responsibility for presenting the fact files of three of the animals each. They should read only their three, underlining key facts to share; then get into a group of three with students who have read about different animals. They then take turns to present the key facts, ranking the animals as they go along.
- After the main task feedback/extension, they can mine their texts for further phrases/structures that seem important. See the suggestions on text-mining in the introduction.
- Follow up the task/language focus by doing one of the following:
  A) Students discuss this topic: *True or False: humans are the most dangerous animal.* Divide the class into two groups. AAA – they find arguments for the motion; BBB – they find arguments against the motion. After a preparation phase, they pair up (AB/AB/AB) and try to persuade their partner of their position.
  B) Fact check: assign an animal to each pair and ask them to search for further facts online, and to see if the facts contained in each text seem to be accurate or oversimplified.
  C) Assign further animals for the students to research on the internet, in order to present findings in terms of how dangerous they are. Possible selection: *rhinoceros, the cobra, the tiger, the puffer fish, the Tsetse Fly, the Golden Poison Dart Frog.*

Language feedback options

- Lexis connected to animal behaviour, facts and dangers: *hunt, predator, prey/victim, territorial, food chain, poison/poisonous/venom*
- Language for contrast and comparison: *although, though, however, while, whereas;* comparative and superlative structures e.g. *the most sociable*
- Describing general/typical behaviour: the present simple, adjectives/adverbs such as *in general, rare/rarely, typical/typically, common/commonly, usually*
- The passive: *a human who is attacked, in danger of being bitten*

▶ How to run the activity

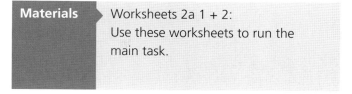

Levels	A2 – B2
Ages	8 – 16
Length	45 minutes

Materials   Worksheets 2a 1 + 2: Use these worksheets to run the main task.

Pre-task

- Play a game of draw, describe, mime to introduce the animals: *snake, snail, shark, polar bear, mosquito, lion, jellyfish, hippopotamus, crocodile*. Put the students into 3 or 4 teams. One person from each team comes to the front and is given one of the animals – they should choose to describe it, draw it on the board or mime it to the rest of their team (variations: 1) they cannot use the same method twice in a row, 2) they roll a dice to decide e.g. 1–2 – describe, 3–4 draw, 5–6 mime). The team that guesses first gets one point. The team with the most points at the end wins.
- Put the name of the animal up on the board each time it is correctly guessed, so that at the end of the activity, all of the animals are there for students to see.

Task 1

- Ask the students in pairs or groups to categorise the animals – *very dangerous, quite dangerous, not dangerous.* They should agree together on this.
- Option: if you have time, ask the students to find a new partner to compare their categories and justify why they placed them there.

Main task

- Tell the students that, in fact, all of the animals are dangerous in some way and they will read some facts about them shortly. Let them know that the facts are about certain types of animal in some cases – for example, a normal garden snail is not dangerous but there is a type of snail that is *very* dangerous.
- Ask them in pairs to decide why each animal could be/is dangerous, noting two or three reasons in the middle column of the worksheet.
- Give the students Dangerous animals 2: ask them to read the facts about these animals. They can underline key words/phrases that indicate why they are dangerous. Then in pairs they can share the one they feel is most dangerous, and least dangerous.
- Feedback on the pairwork briefly before setting the main task: students should form groups of 3 or 4 and, using the information in the text, try to rank the animals from the least to the most dangerous, saying why they think so.
- Option: finish with a plenary session in which all groups contribute their ideas and a ranked list is agreed upon on the board.

Dangerous animals 1

	Why is it dangerous?	Danger rank (1 = most dangerous; 10 = least dangerous)
	The black mamba	
	The hippopotamus	
	The box jellyfish	
	The Great White shark	
	The polar bear	
	The mosquito	
	The saltwater crocodile	
	The lion	
	The cone snail	

ACTIVITIES FOR TASK-BASED LEARNING
by Neil Anderson and Neil McCutcheon
© DELTA Publishing, 2019 | www.deltapublishing.co.uk
ISBN 978-3-12-501701-6

Dangerous animals 2

The black mamba snake	The black mamba is an extremely poisonous snake that lives in many countries in sub-Saharan Africa. It is usually between 2-3 metres long, but it can grow to 4.5 metres. While it doesn't normally attack humans, it can become aggressive if it senses a human within 40 metres. It can move at a speed of about 16 km/h and can bite a standing human on the legs or upper body; its venom is extremely toxic and can kill within 7 hours unless it is treated with antivenom. However, attacks are rare as Black Mambas do not usually live in areas populated by humans.
The hippo-potamus	The hippopotamus – "river horse" - can look peaceful as it relaxes in a river but make no mistake: its behaviour is unpredictable and at times very aggressive. With their sharp 50 cm teeth, 1,500 kg weight and a speed of 19 km/h, they kill up to 500 people a year in Africa. They are territorial, especially when in the water; they will often attack boats that pass by them. Females protecting their young may also attack if they feel threatened. In general, though, hippos prefer to spend their time relaxing in the water during the day and eating about 70 kgs of grass on land at night.
The box jellyfish	The box jellyfish is most commonly found in the Indian Ocean and the Pacific Ocean. Its body is only about 20 cms long, but it has 15 tentacles that are each 3 metres long…and each one has thousands of hooks that can inject poison into their victim! Unlike most jellyfish, they actively hunt, looking for small fish to kill. Although they don't hunt humans, many people have been stung, as the animal is very hard to see in the water. Some of the larger species can kill you in only a few minutes, but most types of box jellyfish are not that dangerous and will only make most human adults very sick.

The Great White shark	The Great White shark is possibly the most feared of all sea creatures: but attacks on humans are very rare, and not always fatal. These 4.5 metre sharks are top of the food chain in the ocean. With their sharp nose and rows of sharper teeth, they hunt from below, and when they sense prey, they swim suddenly towards it, mouths open wide. Although attacks are not usually fatal, a single bite can easily kill a human; and even if the victim survives the bite, blood loss and shock can finish the job. But remember: this doesn't happen often, and they don't actively hunt for humans.
The polar bear	The polar bear is top of the food chain in the Arctic Circle: this fantastic creature can weigh up to 700 kgs and is able to smell its prey from 1 km away. It can swim for days at a time as it searches for food, and you probably won't see it until it is too late: it hunts seals (its favourite food) quietly, moving slowly and low in the snow. Attacks on humans are rare but melting ice means contact between humans and bears is increasing, as the bears move to populated areas. A polar bear will certainly try to kill any human it meets. However, climate change is making it much harder for bears to find food, and the polar bear population is decreasing in size.
The mosquito	The mosquito is tiny but possibly the most dangerous animal of all: although most mosquitoes do not bite humans (as they prefer the blood of other animals), they still kill more humans than any other animal – approximately 830,000 people per year. The main problem is the diseases passed on to humans through mosquito bites: the Zika virus, yellow fever, dengue fever and, above all, malaria. While mosquitoes are particularly problematic in tropical areas, around 50% of the world's population are in danger of being bitten by a diseased mosquito.

The salt-water crocodile	The saltwater crocodile is the largest of all reptiles, with males typically being 6 metres long and 100 kgs in weight. They are found in Asia and Australia, in more places than any other type of crocodile, and the really bad news is they are more likely to hunt and attach humans than any other type of reptile. Because of their size and speed, a human who is attacked by one is unlikely to survive. Although other crocodiles such as the Nile crocodile in Egypt live closer to human populations, none are more aggressive than large male saltwater crocodiles – apart from their teeth, they can smash prey with their heads and tails.
The lion	The lion is the most sociable of big cats, living and hunting in "prides" of up to 15 related animals. Prides cooperate as they hunt, increasing their chance of catching prey that are very fast (e.g. gazelles) or very large (e.g. giraffes). In general, the smaller lioness does the work during a group hunt, with males typically not participating. When the prey is caught, they will usually strangle it until it cannot breathe, and then eat most of the victim where the kill happened; they need 5–7 kgs of meat every day. Lions are "apex" predators: they hunt but are not hunted by any other animal…except, of course, humans.
The cone snail	Why is a snail on the list of most dangerous animals? This is the cone snail, no ordinary snail. It usually lives in coral reefs in warm tropical waters such as the Pacific and Caribbean. They hunt small fish, worms and other snails, and you are not likely to meet one if you are just swimming or snorkelling near the surface of the sea. However, the cone snail has been known to kill divers who pick them up, attracted by their beautiful shells. They attack by shooting a poison tooth into victims; this can be very painful if the snail is smaller, or fatal in the case of the larger types. Many divers who wish to sell the pretty shells for jewellery die before they have the chance to.

© DELTA Publishing, 2019 | www.deltapublishing.co.uk
ISBN 978-3-12-501701-6

ACTIVITIES FOR TASK-BASED LEARNING
by Neil Anderson and Neil McCutcheon

2d Me not me

 About the activity

Task type	Sorting/categorising
Task outcome	Students categorise ideas and objects according to personal feeling and association, comparing views with a partner.

Introduction

This activity is simple but effective: students decide how they feel about given words, ideas or objects, and then explain why, comparing with a partner. As it is so straightforward, it can be used as a lead-in to any topic in the coursebook; for more extended fluency practice; or even to review vocabulary.

Variation, extension, task repetition

- If you have more time and students remain motivated, after the pairwork, ask them to mingle/work in a ladder, and to talk to at least three different people. Their goal is to listen to each partner's day and decide who they would like to spend the day with.
- Note that **Me not me** is really a frame for personalisation and it is endlessly flexible in terms of content. The words dictated could be:
  - Words connected to the topic of a lesson in the lead-in – it works with most topics common to coursebooks e.g. holidays, family, work.
  - Words being recycled from recent lessons, with students making personal associations such as how this concept applies to them, or to what extent they like/dislike the word.

Sample activities to dictate		
stay at home/lie in bed	visit the zoo	cook a fancy meal
plan for the next day	catch up on housework	people watch in a cafe
take a day trip to another town	do something adventurous	visit an old friend
go to the gym	go to work anyway	go for a long drive

Language feedback options

- Hypothetical language: *I'd stay at home… I'd love to… If I had a car, I'd.*
- Likes/dislikes, abilities and preferences: *I can't stand sitting around; I'd rather be active… I can't cook so that wouldn't be possible… I'm not a fan of…*
- Asking for/giving reasons and justifying choices: *Why did you put it there? I think this is "Not Me" as…*
- Note that, depending on how the activity is set up, instead of a hypothetical frame, it can be used for present tenses (things that are generally true of each student), past tenses (e.g. what they did last weekend or holiday) or future forms (e.g. plans for the weekend, or next holiday).
- Lexis related to the topic selected – any topic appropriate to giving opinions and stating preferences.

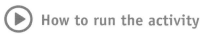 **How to run the activity**

Levels	A2–C1
Ages	all
Length	Flexible: 10–45 minutes

Materials	Worksheet 2d
	Whiteboard / board / projector

Pre-task

- Tell the students you have unexpectedly been given a day off in the near future. Ask them in pairs to think of three things they imagine you will do on this day off and things they feel you will not do e.g. *spend the day on the sofa; go to a museum; visit loved ones.*
- As a visual prompt, draw a cline on the board, with *Me* on one end and *Not Me* on the other, as below:

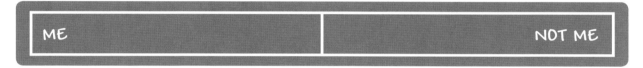

ME   NOT ME

- Listen to student ideas and place them along the bottom axis, according to how likely you are to do these things. Explain why you think these activities are "me" or "not me".

Main task

- Tell students they will now imagine they have a day off next week. You will dictate a number of possible activities they could do during this day, and they need to place them on the cline. If it is something they would very likely do, then they can place it towards the left; if it is something they are very unlikely to do, then they should place it on the right. Let them know they can place these ideas *anywhere* on the cline, depending on their personal feelings about it – they shouldn't just cluster on the two poles.
- Use the worksheet or ask the students to copy the cline into their notebooks, leaving enough space to write a number of activities along the horizontal axis.
- Dictate a number of possible free time activities (see the box above for some ideas; these prompts should be scaled to the level of the students). Ideally, these will be a range of the more typical – even mundane – to the more unusual and even exotic. Tailor this to your group in order to elicit a range of responses to each idea. The students place them and then prepare to share and explain why.
- In pairs, students take turns to name one of the activities, saying where they placed it and why. The outcome here is to find similarities and differences from their partner, as well as to elicit more details concerning their feelings about the activity, and what exactly they would do. The instructions can emphasise this – *find two areas where you agree and two areas where you have different preferences.*
- Feedback – ask the students to report back on this, summarising key similarities and differences from their partner.

2d Me not me – the cline

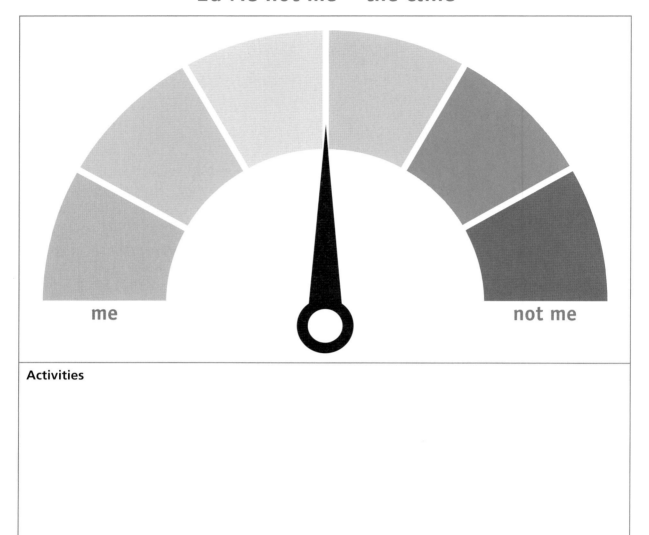

me

not me

Activities

Similarities	Differences

ACTIVITIES FOR TASK-BASED LEARNING
by Neil Anderson and Neil McCutcheon

© DELTA Publishing, 2019 | www.deltapublishing.co.uk
ISBN 978-3-12-501701-6

DELTA Publishing

2e My neighbourhood

 About the activity

Task type	Listing/ranking
Task outcome	Students identify, itemise and evaluate positive/negative features of a neighbourhood.

Introduction

We generally prefer tasks that involve students reflecting on their lives positively: it's common sense that an upbeat atmosphere in the classroom provides better conditions for learning. Sometimes, however, it's good to get things off your chest. Gently (or otherwise) complaining is a fundamental, authentic communicative act: it makes good pedagogical sense to provide our students with the chance to do so in English! This task asks students to consider the downsides to where they live, listing the elements of their immediate neighbourhood (or broader area) that they find less appealing.

Variations and extension

- This doesn't have to be about a neighbourhood – if it feels more appropriate and gives more scope for discussion, broaden the focus so it is about a whole town or city.
- If you feel your students would prefer to keep things positive, make the pre-task the focus of the main task i.e. have them focus on what they love about where they live.
- If the topic feels too personal, then it can be "de-personalised": focus on generic features of a good/bad neighbourhood.
- After the task, as the language focus, have the students look at the email on worksheet 2.
  They can read it for content (e.g. *would you like to live there?*) before picking out phrases related to the suggested language focus areas. See the suggestions on text-mining in the introduction.

Language feedback options

- Lexis for negatively describing a neighbourhood: *polluted, noisy, boring, they make too much noise, they don't mind their own business:*
- Expressing limitations: *…there's a lack of… there are (far) too many…*
- Language for expressing dislikes: *I can't stand… I'm not a fan of… X really irritates/annoys me.*
- Post-modification of the noun, notably relative and participles clauses: *cyclists* <u>riding on the pavement</u> *annoy me; people* <u>who don't switch off their phones</u>

(▶) **How to run the activity**

Levels	B1–C1
Ages	teens and adults
Length	30–45 minutes

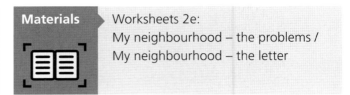

Materials Worksheets 2e:
My neighbourhood – the problems /
My neighbourhood – the letter

Pre-task

- Elicit *local area / neighbourhood* by offering a definition or examples from your city.
- Tell students which part of your town you live in. If possible, show them on google maps, or using physical map. Ask them to guess what you enjoy about living in this neighbourhood. Listen to their ideas, and where appropriate elaborate on what they have said e.g. *You mean the location is convenient? That's true as I can walk into the centre of town in about 10 minutes.*
- Ask the students in pairs to identify what they enjoy about where they live, and to see if they can find anything in common with their partner about the positives of their respective neighbourhoods. Monitor for ideas to focus on in feedback.
- Feedback briefly on what they found in common. Ask what seems most attractive about their partner's neighbourhood that is different from their own (e.g. *what is one thing you like about your partner's neighbourhood that is not true of your neighbourhood?).*

Main task

- Segue to the main task by asking: *do you like <u>everything</u> about your neighbourhood? Do you think <u>I</u> like everything about <u>my</u> neighbourhood?*
- Tell students you are going to look at some things that are less attractive in a neighbourhood. Give students the picture: fold worksheet 1 so they can only see the pictures not the key. Ask them in pairs to look at them one by one and to identify what each "dislike" is. Feedback on this by eliciting the ideas onto the whiteboard in the form of a mind-map. Ask the students to add three or four other areas.
- Ask them to prepare to talk about what they don't enjoy about where they live. They can use the ideas from the pictures / board, making a note in the **My list** column on the worksheet. They should be prepared to talk to each partner for one or two minutes explaining why these things annoy them. Emphasise the listener should find out as much specific information as possible about the annoyance. **Goal:** each student will speak / listen to at least three other students and in feedback the class will agree on the most common annoyances, as well as anything more unusual they heard from a partner.
- Set up a ladder or a mingle and give the students a time limit for the task – about 9 or 10 minutes. Every few minutes, give a signal to ensure the students move on to a new partner. Monitor and identify any good or defective examples of language from the **language feedback options** list.
- Content feedback: focus on the goal. Have students report the most common complaints and anything more unusual they heard. Then move to language focus.

2e My neighbourhood – the problems

	Answer key	My list
1	pollution/dirt	
2	noise from the street/noisy neighbours	
3	lack of green spaces	
4	unfriendly local people	
5	cyclists on the pavement	
6	irresponsible dog owners	

© DELTA Publishing, 2019 | www.deltapublishing.co.uk ISBN 978-3-12-501701-6 ACTIVITIES FOR TASK-BASED LEARNING by Neil Anderson and Neil McCutcheon

2e My neighbourhood – the letter

Hi Paul,

Thanks for the message – glad it's going so well for you! Thanks also for asking about the move and the new flat. It's been about two months since I moved to József Körút and I think I've got a pretty good feel for the local area.

First, the good things: it's pretty great living so close to the centre of town. I can basically get anywhere in central Pest on foot within about 10/15 minutes; and if I'm feeling lazy I can get around by metro or tram. The neighbours directly next door have been really welcoming; they've gone out of their way to make us feel at home, and have helped introduce us to some of the people we need to know here e.g. the "közös képviselő" who is in charge of maintenance for the building. There are a tonne of shops – not just a small mall and supermarket, but around the corner there's a traditional market, and even an Asian supermarket. And we've got a lot of pubs and cafes to choose from ☺.

It's not perfect though! You asked if there was anything worse here than across the river, and there a few things that irritate me about the area...

- it's pretty noisy, and polluted – it's difficult to get used to the tram thundering past, shaking the windows (even though we're on the third floor). The downside to having plenty of pubs around is the noise that revellers make at night, especially if we leave the windows open.
- Dogs. Really. Or rather, dog-owners treating the pavement like it's a toilet for their pets. I can't stand it when people don't clean up after their dogs – it sometimes feels like you are stepping out into a minefield. Also, everyone seems to have at least one if not more dogs in their flats, barking all day long.
- We live on a busy road, with a lot of traffic, so I don't want to seem unfair but, seriously, cyclists riding on the pavement drive me mad. I know it's safer for them than being on the road and most of them are careful but I've nearly been knocked over at least twice.
- It's great being in the centre but there's a lack of green spaces – the nearest decent park is about half an hour away. It can feel a bit too "built up" sometimes to be honest, and the best thing about the old neighbourhood was the park within walking distance of our flat.
- One last thing: some of our neighbours are nice, but there are quite a few who are less welcoming. It bothers me that some of them don't look at me or reply when I say good morning, good afternoon etc. What's that all about?

Enough moaning! It's a good neighbourhood overall. I hope I haven't put you off visiting – when are you going to come over??

Catch you soon,

Neil

ACTIVITIES FOR TASK-BASED LEARNING
by Neil Anderson and Neil McCutcheon

© DELTA Publishing, 2019 | www.deltapublishing.co.uk
ISBN 978-3-12-501701-6

2f Speed flatmating

 About the activity

Task type	carousel/ladder discussion
Task outcome	Students first discuss and rank the qualities they would like to find in an ideal flatmate, then interview other members of the class to find an ideal match.

Introduction

"How often does a house need to be cleaned, anyway? As a general rule, once every girlfriend." P. J. O' Rourke. We have all experienced a measure of domestic disharmony with family members or flatmates, and most people have an idea of the kind of flat – or housemate they would "fit" best with. This version of an EFL classic can easily function as a get-to-know-you activity at the beginning of new courses. The teens adaptation is an idea from a colleague, Alan Weir.

Variation, extension, task repetition

One obvious variation – and one that is usually a great success in creating conversation – is speed-dating, in which students look for an ideal partner.

- With teenage groups, who may be uncomfortable with the subject-matter, students can be in role as made-up or celebrities and fictional characters (James Bond, Beyoncé, Doctor Who – whoever is current) of their own or the opposite sex. Add a dash of humour by getting them to write "hot" or "not" against the identities of the people they meet. One option is to get them to write down their names and their three favourite "dates" at the end and put these into a hat. The slips can then be shared out among the small groups, who try and find perfect matches.
- Another variation, if you need to be less personal, is match-making/friend-finding. Students first think of a single friend, and write down their qualities, of course accentuating the positive ones. (There is a chance for some initial language feedback at this point.) They then mingle as above, but in this version they are looking for a suitable potential date for their friend.

Language feedback options

Question forms arise throughout the activity, and this is an area of language where all levels benefit from feedback.

- Modal /semi-modal verbs: the best candidate *should/has to be someone who likes* etc.
- Adjectives to describe personality: *easygoing, laid-back, well-organised, considerate…*
- Language to compare and contrast candidates: comparatives, superlatives. X is more likely to, less tidy than
- Quantifiers: *too* + adj, *not* + adj *enough*, *not all that* + adj

▶ **How to run the activity**

Levels	A2–C2
Ages	teens, young adult
Length	30–40 minutes

Materials	Worksheet 2f

Pre-task

- Showing the students a short clip of a programme featuring flatmates, such as **Friends**, can be a good way into this topic. The opening scene from the film **Shallow Grave**, in which potential flatmates are interviewed, and in fact "grilled", can work with higher level groups.
- Ask students what things are important to them when assessing the suitability of new flatmates.
- One option is to use this to create a class list and get pairs to rank what are, for them, the most important qualities of an *ideal* flatmate. Tell the pairs that they should try and agree on the most important ones, and report back.

Task

- Students are told that they have the responsibility for interviewing candidates for new flatmates. This can be done individually or, if you have a large class, in pairs or small groups – the people in the flatshare.
- First, based on the ideas from earlier, they write down some questions to ask the prospective flatmates.
- One option is to have some initial language feedback at this stage – by getting students to write their questions on the whiteboard. This is particularly worth doing for lower levels.
- The main part of the activity, one-to-one interviews, now takes place. Students sit in pairs and move round in a kind of "carousel" arrangement (outer and inner circle) or at desks. It's a good idea to have an approximate time-limit, for example 2 minutes each way. Higher level students may wish to have longer.
- Students take notes as they go.
- After students have talked to a number of prospective flatmates, they decide who the best candidate is and report back in groups. (For the flatshare groups, they must reconvene and come to a group decision.)

2f Speed flatmating – the interviews

You need to find out about your potential new flatmates. Ask questions to find out if you could share a flat with this person. You have .... minutes with each person.

Names:	1.	2.	3.
tidy/untidy?			
dishes?			
pets?			
food preferences?			
loud music?			
introvert, extrovert?			
parties?			

Names:	4.	5.	6.
tidy/untidy?			
dishes?			
pets?			
food preferences?			
loud music?			
introvert, extrovert?			
parties?			

© DELTA Publishing, 2019 | www.deltapublishing.co.uk
ISBN 978-3-12-501701-6
ACTIVITIES FOR TASK-BASED LEARNING
by Neil Anderson and Neil McCutcheon

3 Opinions

3a How strict were your parents?

 About the activity

Task type	information gap
Task outcome	Students find out who in the class had the strictest/most lenient parents.

Introduction

This is a well-established task, and one which was mentioned by Jane and Dave Willis in their book, **Doing Task-Based Teaching**. The subject is one that is perennially interesting, whatever the age of the students. With older students, we tilt the initial discussion towards the idea that children may be less disciplined than in the past, and with teenagers it can be framed to reflect their own thoughts and concerns in the present. We have always found that groups are willing to contribute personal information, but to avoid any awkwardness in the interviews, we teach an option such as "I'd rather not say", which must be respected.

Variation, extension, text repetition

A good discussion is for the students to talk about what their own approach to parenting would be, or (if they are parents) to reflect on their own rewards, rules and punishments. You can ask students if they have a similar or different approach to that of their own parents. In order to **capture** the language here, you may want to ask students to write down some of these ideas. To make this more communicative, pairs or small groups can agree on a list of rules. For lower level groups, the focus here can be narrowed to modals and real conditionals e.g. *If you want to keep getting your pocket money, you must tidy your room.*

Language feedback options

The most obvious area to focus on is the language of obligation, including verb complementation (verb patterns). Some genuine examples that arose in the recording were:

> *"They <u>made me get</u> a job in a pub."*
> *"My parents didn't <u>let me go</u>."*
> *"It was <u>not allowed</u>."*
> *"I was <u>made to go out</u> and <u>get</u> a job."*
> *"I don't know if they <u>threatened me with something</u>."*

This can be narrowed to a more tightly controlled focus on *make, let, allow, force, encourage, ask, tell, want somebody (to)* + *V* (and the respective passive forms) and/or lexis to describe obligation: *compulsory, forbidden, obliged to, had to, didn't have to*. Indirect speech vocabulary and structures can emerge.

Other vocabulary of interest on the accompanying recording was: *rules and regulations, zero tolerance, adamant that, slave labour, lived in fear…*

How to run the activity

Levels	B1+
Ages	all ages
Length	1 hour +

Materials	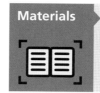 Worksheet 3a: You may also want to bring some photographs of your own family to help you talke about your own experiences.

Pre-task

To lead into the topic, you could show the students a picture from your childhood, or a generic stock picture. You could begin with an anecdote from this time, or from your teenage years to establish the context. (e.g. as a teenager, you were forbidden to have parties at home when your parents were away for short periods.) Students often ask questions at this stage, and this is a good opportunity just to talk.

- Some topic-related items we elicit at this stage are *strict, lenient, pocket money, punishments, naughty* and *well-behaved*.
- With lower level groups, you may wish to pre-teach lexis for household chores.
- Give students the questionnaire below, and give them a few minutes to think about their own answers to the questions. You can vary the questionnaire as appropriate, depending on cultural circumstances and how well the students know each other. Some questions, about parties, chores or pocket-money, may be narrowed by age. More creative students can create their *own* questions, given one or two prompts, which can then be harvested and provided to the group using the whiteboard or dictation.

Task

- Instruct task. The students have to interview each other using some or all of the questions. This can be done in various ways, for example interviewing a partner (using all the questions) to find out whose parents were *stricter*. Another format is "mingling", where each student has one question and polls everyone in the class to find out whose parents were strict or lenient.
- Demonstrate with a student to give everyone an approximate idea of the length of turns you expect, and to encourage follow-up questions too.
- Tell students that they should take notes as they need to keep the goal in mind, and there will be some reporting back to do!
- Early finishers can work with these notes to prepare their report.
- Ensure there is a good content feedback stage now – students will inevitably be very interested in the results of the interviews/survey. Try to use your monitoring of the task to focus some of the content feedback.

Post-task

We often play a short recording of one of us and a colleague doing the same task. This is set with a simple "gist" task – *which of us had stricter parents?* The recording here is rich with language to focus on explicitly at the next stage: grammar, vocabulary and common discourse markers. (If you prefer a more traditional approach, this recording may be used earlier in the lesson.)

3a How strict were your parents? – a questionnaire

Use these, or similar questions, to find out about how strict other students' parents were.

a) Do you think your parents were strict or lenient?

b) Did they allow you to come home late?

c) When you went out did you always have to tell them where you were going?

d) Did they let you have parties at their house?

e) Did your parents make you do chores/housework?

f) How much pocket money did you get?

g) Were you ever punished?

My parents were always really strict.

I was never allowed to have a party.

My parents let me come and go as I wanted.

ACTIVITIES FOR TASK-BASED LEARNING
by Neil Anderson and Neil McCutcheon

© DELTA Publishing, 2019 | www.deltapublishing.co.uk
ISBN 978-3-12-501701-6

3b Polarities + Opinion gallery

 About the activity

Task type	opinion gap
Task outcome	Students will give reasons to support their opinions, and share these with others to find areas of agreement and disagreement.

Introduction

Controversy works to generate language, because there is a natural communicative need to explain and justify your opinion. It's important to choose the right topics. They should be controversial enough to divide people but not so much so that you start "culture wars" in your classroom. (See also the task called **This House Believes** in this section.) Polarities works well as a warmer, and the **Opinion Gallery** is a task that will take a longer.

Variation, extension, task repetition

- Students can think of their own provocative statements to extend either activity here.
- Dictation. The controversial statements can be used as a kind of mini-dictogloss (See the final chapter **Whole class**). Instead of labelling the statements on display with letters, provide a word or two to summarise each one. Before students discuss their attitudes, they co-operate to reconstruct the original statement.
- "Steel-manning" your opponent. Students have to take another student's point of view and express it in a way that does full justice to the other person's point of view.

Language feedback options

- Starting out: *OK, What do you think about…? What's your opinion/view about…?*
- Stating one's opinion *in my opinion, in my view, I think that, the (main/ most important) thing is, One thing to bear in mind is, What I think/feel is…*
- Agreeing: *Exactly, I (fully) agree, I agree wholeheartedly, That's exactly what I think, You're bang on, You're so right (about that)*
- Partially agreeing: *I half agree, I don't fully agree, I get that/the point about, but…, I know what you mean, but…, I'm with you to some extent, I want to agree, but…*
- Disagreeing: *Not at all! Oh, come on/come off it! That's nonsense! Rubbish!*
- Contradicting: *It's no good saying that… It's the exact opposite.*
- Softening: *With respect, I see what you mean but…, Perhaps/Maybe, I find that…, I tend to think that…*
- Disjuncts to show the speaker's attitude: *Honestly, frankly, Hopefully, To tell the truth, To be frank/honest (with you)*
- Generalising: *On the whole, in general, This is a huge generalisation, but…, Overall*
- Efforts to persuade: *You've got to admit that, You must see that, After all*
- Conceding points: *However, All the same, nevertheless, it's probably true that…*
- Referring and focusing adverbials: *Regarding, As far as X is/are concerned, In fact, Actually, In actual fact, I mean, In other words*
- Linkers to add ideas (*another thing is…*) and make contrasting points (*even so, That's all very well, but…*)
- Finishing: *So we agree then! Let's agree to differ*

▶ How to run the activity

			Materials	Worksheets 3b
Levels	▸	A2–C2		Examples of "polarities" and short
Ages	▸	any		controversial statements
Length	▸	10–40 minutes		

Task 1 (Polarities)

You will need a list of statements which have the potential to cleave your class into two equally-sized groups. For the best results, keep the statements quite light-hearted, though some students may prefer more thought-provoking ones. Examples are provided on the list below. Obviously, choose ones that are suitable for your students; if possible, you can link the topic to the broader topic of your lesson, or use it to review a topic you have recently covered.

- Draw a scale on the board and put different options – you can use the examples here – at opposite ends. Students have to think about which kind of person they are – they should go with their first answer, and no "fence-sitting" is allowed.
- Students walk to different sides of the room, depending on their response, so that they are now together with their own "side". Now they brainstorm arguments to support their opinions.
- Next, they pair off with someone with a *different* opinion and repeat some of these reasons. (If one side outnumbers the other, this is all right. You will simply have to direct more to form the recombined groups.) The students can try to persuade their partner from the opposite side, try to win the argument, or just agree to differ. We like to leave these options open, as these are mostly matters of personal inclination.
- Elicit some of the reasons in feedback, or ask students to write down something about their opposite's opinions (See "steel-manning" above) for feedback later.

Task 2 (Opinion gallery):

- You need a list of reasonably controversial statements, such as the ones to the left. Display these around the walls of the classroom. It's a good idea to label them with letters of the alphabet them for convenient reference later.
- Students walk round individually, read each statement and on their own notepaper they should write next to the letter for each one a number 1–10 indicating how they feel about it. 10 = *I completely agree with this.* 1 = *I totally disagree.*
- Now students sit in pairs or small groups, find the statements they most disagree about and discuss these. Again, as above, there is no pressure to reach a conclusion. They can try to persuade the others in the group, or agree to differ.
- Encourage students to write down one of the opinions of someone else in the group, for a plenary feedback stage.

3b Opinion gallery – opinions

For each of the statements you see, write a number here to represent what you think.
10 = *I completely agree with this.* 1 = *I totally disagree.*

	My opinion	**Reconstruct the controversial statement**
stay at home		It is better for children's development if one parent can stay at home to take care of them.
basic income		
free speech		
lies		
human rights		
world government		
crimes / decades		
time online		
climate change		
religious education		
dating		
salary		

ACTIVITIES FOR TASK-BASED LEARNING
by Neil Anderson and Neil McCutcheon

3b Opinion gallery – the controversial statements

- It is better for children's development if one parent can stay at home to take care of them.
- The time has come for a universal basic income.
- There should be no limits to freedom of speech, except in cases of hate speech.
- Parents should never lie to children./Doctors should never lie to patients.
- The idea of human rights is Eurocentric and should not be imposed on other cultures.
- A world government is a good idea.
- People should not be put on trial for crimes decades after they were committed.
- The amount of time children spend online should be rationed.
- Climate change denial should be a crime.
- Religious education ought to be banned. (NB Do not use this one if not culturally appropriate!)
- It is all right for a man to date a much younger woman, but not the other way round.
- There should be a maximum salary in the public sector: the Prime Minister's.

3b Polarities: What is more you...?

Circle the option that is more you. Don't think about it for too long – just go with your instinct.

Mac	**PC**
sweet	**savoury**
indoors	**outdoors**
tea	**coffee**
CD or MP3	**vinyl or MP3**
Facebook	**Twitter**
driving	**taking the train**
giving	**receiving**
pop	**classical**
introvert	**extrovert**
realist	**idealist**
early bird	**night owl**
cat person	**dog person**

ACTIVITIES FOR TASK-BASED LEARNING
by Neil Anderson and Neil McCutcheon

© DELTA Publishing, 2019 | www.deltapublishing.co.uk
ISBN 978-3-12-501701-6

3c Counsellors / Dilemmas

 About the activity

Task type	role-play (service provider and client)
Task outcome	Students will discuss some life problems with others in the class, and decide on the best advice.

Introduction

A problem shared is a problem halved; dilemmas and problems are ideal opportunities for students to think creatively and to communicate. While describing the problem may be less demanding, and within the range of pre-intermediate students, creating and evaluating solutions are higher-order thinking skills and will generate more complex language at higher levels. The "carousel" framework (See **1 Micro-strategies**) for the role-play activity is a classic. It can be varied to fit different contexts, some of which are listed below.

Variation, extension, task repetition

- Landlords looking for tenants. (See **6b Home exchange**).
- Travellers looking for holiday destinations, and holiday company representatives.
- Careers guidance interviews, or job fairs, in which prospective employees sell their skills to employers.

Language feedback options

- Clearly, the language of advice and making suggestions is going to be required. If students already know *should*, be ready with variations, for instance *Why not + V? You could always + V. Have you thought of + Ving? One idea is to + V, It might be worth = Ving, It's worth a try*
- Students will have to state their problems clearly and you could input some sentence heads such as: *the (main) thing / problem / difficulty is… I'm not sure how to…*
- Any language explaining reasons and results, and to respond to advice: *the reason why… the problem with X is that, X leads to / tends to, That's not a bad idea, I might take you up on that*
- Conditionals type 1 and 2 for discussing the results: *If you do X, you might well find that …*
- Asking for clarification: *Can you say that again? I'm not sure exactly what you mean by*

What's the problem?	
Who does it involve?	
Why did it happen?	
What are you thinking about doing?	
What might the consequences be?	

▶ How to run the activity

Levels	A2–C2
Ages	teens, young adult
Length	45 minutes +

Materials	Slips of paper for students to write their problems on An envelope You may need one or two pre-prepared problems.

Pre-task

- It's a good idea for the teacher to begin with a problem of his/her own. Sharing this kind of personal material makes students more comfortable with doing the same thing. We recommend starting with something lighter, such as that you have a phobia of spiders, or fear of flying. Whatever you choose, the idea is for students to brainstorm advice for you in groups, and then to present this.
- You can then now listen to the groups' ideas, which will possibly include some surreal and humorous suggestions, as well as sound advice, and choose your favourite ones. (Other students can listen, do the same, and see whether they agree with you in the end.)

Main task

- First, tell the students they are going to write a real problem of theirs (or a friend's) on one of the slips of paper. Tell them it should be a real problem, though it needn't be a serious problem. They should describe it concisely, though providing enough detail so that the solutions can be concrete. (You will have to circulate and support with vocabulary at this point, and you have the option of following this stage with some feedback on any language that has arisen.)
- Put the problems in a hat or envelope. Students get to pick one out, making sure that it is not their own. Allow students a minute or two to ask any questions about anything in the description that they don't understand.
- Arrange the class into a "carousel" with an inner and outer circle of chairs. Tell them that they will be counsellors and their clients. The students will be moving from partner to partner.
- In pairs, the client reads their problem to the counsellor as if it is his/her own. The counsellor can ask questions to find out more information, which the client may have to make up. (This is why real problems are better.) Then they need to provide advice.
- At your signal, students move on to the next counsellor and repeat the process. This can be done a number of times with larger classes.
- Students now swap roles, so that the counsellors are the new clients.
- When everyone has had enough time to talk, the students should decide which solution is best to "their" problem. You should ask them to report back. If you allow some preparation time, students can make notes and provide a more considered (and accurate) report. Some of these reports may generate further discussion in the open class.

3d Tenancy agreement

 About the activity

Task type	role-play
Task outcome	Students will participate in a dialogue as landlords and prospective tenants, and finalise a tenancy agreement.

Introduction

This task can be run with **4a Bad neighbours** as an opening task or a follow-up, as they are both about a similar theme. It can also stand alone as a **focused task**, which is bound to generate modal verbs. The theme is one that most people can relate to: the sometimes strained relationship between landlords and tenants. Whatever their previous experience, students enjoy being on both sides of this role-play, and produce plenty of ideas, which lead to some humorous results.

Variation, extension, task repetition

- One very successful variation of a similar role-play which pits strict parents against recalcitrant teenagers; this may culminate in an informal written "contract". Lead in with a general discussion about the kinds of things teenagers want, and restrictions parents may want to impose. Next, students in role as parents and teenagers decide on their demands: "red lines" and areas where they might be persuaded to compromise.

Language feedback options

This is a so-called focused task as it is easy to predict beforehand exactly which language is likely to arise in this context. Modal and semi-modal auxiliary verbs, especially to do with permission and obligation: *Can we have pets? You mustn't have noisy parties. Will you repaint the living room? You have to pay the local tax. We don't have to pay the water bills.*
- Functional language for requests: *Would it be possible to…? Would you mind if I…? Could you just…?*
- Other vocabulary to do with the same notions of obligation and permission: *We're allowed to sub-let; It's forbidden to smoke in the flat.*
- All kinds of real conditionals, which will include the first conditional, also with other conjunctions such as *unless* and *provided/providing that: I'll agree not to raise the rent in the first year as long as you keep the flat clean and tidy.* Note that the language of conditionality does not always follow the conventional patterns isolated in textbooks: *Do that and you're out!*
- Relevant adjectives to describe personality: *demanding, unreasonable, untidy, irresponsible, fussy*
- Possibly you might introduce some more formal language for the actual "contracts": *The landlord shall provide… The tenant may… X is obliged to…*

How to run the activity

Levels	A2+
Ages	adult (and a Young Learners' variation)
Length	45 minutes

Materials	Worksheet 3d

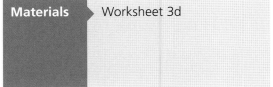

Pre-task

- Pre-teach key words like *landlord, tenant, rent, deposit, sub-let…*
- To set the context, tell the students about an apartment you have stayed in, and what the terms and conditions were – emphasise whether you think you have (or had) a good deal in terms of things that you are allowed to do. For example: *My landlady never seems to be around and spends at least six months in another country. She didn't make a fuss about replacing the boiler, but on the other hand she hasn't replaced the broken intercom. The amount I pay for rent hasn't changed in 5 years…*
- If you want to add a dramatic element, you can show a picture of a rather fierce-looking "landlord" and an unkempt and sloppy-looking tenant.

Main task

- Brainstorm the kinds of things that tenants might want to ask about – for example, are they allowed to have pets, redecorate, have parties, or sub-let the flat?
- Divide the class into landlords and tenants, who now have to produce a list of their requests/and terms & conditions respectively. Students can work in pairs to pool their ideas; this is often a fun stage of the lesson as they get into character and come up with unreasonable demands.
- Now pair the students off: one landlord with one tenant. (You may prefer to have each landlord negotiate with pairs or small groups of tenants, especially if you have an odd number of students in the class.) Tell them that they have to reach some kind of agreement – if not, the landlord will have trouble finding someone else for a while, and the tenants will be on the street. Give them a time-limit.
- At the end of the time allocated, each side could produce a "contract" in which they try as accurately and fairly as they can to represent what they have heard from their interlocutor. Then they can exchange contracts to find out whether they are both happy with the final result!

3d Tenancy agreement – the expectations + the contract

Landlords	Tenants
We want..	We want……

The tenancy contract

We have agreed that...

© DELTA Publishing, 2019 | www.deltapublishing.co.uk
ISBN 978-3-12-501701-6 ACTIVITIES FOR TASK-BASED LEARNING
by Neil Anderson and Neil McCutcheon

61

3e This house believes...

 About the activity

Task type	opinion gap
Task outcome	Students will participate in a debate, and vote on the motion.

Introduction

Debates are a popular activity with students, including some opinionated adolescents we have worked with! Because students are called on to think in a more abstract way, or at least to provide reasons to support their arguments, this is potentially a high-demand activity that can be exploited to focus on linguistic complexity. One organisational challenge is making sure that everyone is involved at every stage in the debate. The choice of topic is obviously important too: see below for some suggested topics. It's really important to choose something students are interested in and that is culturally appropriate.

Variation, extension, task repetition

- One option is to record the main speakers during the debate to help **capture** relevant language that arises.
- One option is to use a short text, especially if your students have trouble generating their own ideas. Students can be asked to what extent they agree with the writer's view.

Language feedback options

- See 3b.

How to run the activity

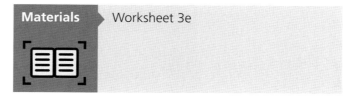

Levels	B1–C2
Ages	teens, young adult
Length	45 minutes +

Materials	Worksheet 3e

Pre-task

- The more controversial you can be at this point, the better. Get students thinking about the topic *without going too deeply into their opinions* at this stage. You may want to use some visual stimuli here.

Main task

- Group students into opposing teams. You have a choice here: group students according to their real opinions or at random.
- Groups should work together to produce ideas both in favour and against the motion. They should do this in note form. It may be helpful to give them the worksheet.
- Groups should also choose a proposer and a seconder. With lower levels, the chosen speakers can share the arguments between them so that each is responsible for their own points. With higher levels, the second speaker can be encouraged to respond to points she has heard from the opposing team.
- It is now time to run the debate: the speaker and seconder from each team speak, as you moderate.
- Move on to the question and discussion stage. One trick you might want to try is to give each student five coins. They can put them down if they ask a question (to one of the speakers) or make a point from the floor. The objective is for everyone to get rid of all their coins. This stage can last as long as the students are coming up with ideas. If you are able to, you could also give them different coloured cards. This shows nicely who's been actively participating!

More debate topics

- Children should be banned from having smart phones.
- It is wrong for the governments to have access to people's phone calls and emails.
- Downloading and copying MP3s and films is theft.
- There should be a limit to what sports stars/entertainers can earn.
- We should all stop eating factory-farmed meat and become vegetarian.
- Recreational drug use should be legalised.
- Use the song *The Winner Takes it All* by perennial favourites ABBA to introduce the idea of Fate versus Fortune. Is it all "meant to be" or do the gods roll a dice? (You should find your adult classes split quite easily into believers and non-believers in Fate, and this can lead to a very productive discussion.)

3e This house believes...

... that social media has done more harm than good.

> *Social media is a modern addiction, especially for the generation called "millennials". So many people sit around all the time staring at illuminated screens that they fail to notice what is going all around them. Wake up, people! You need to take a break and check out the real world for a minute. Life is more than your next post – you could be having a real conversation. Spending so much time online, competing for likes, doctoring our photos to make our lives appear perfect, is actually making us depressed and preventing us from cultivating real relationships.*

Arguments in favour	Arguments against
Counterarguments expected	**Counterarguments expected**
Responses to counterarguments	**Responses to counterarguments**

ACTIVITIES FOR TASK-BASED LEARNING
by Neil Anderson and Neil McCutcheon
© DELTA Publishing, 2019 | www.deltapublishing.co.uk
ISBN 978-3-12-501701-6

DELTA Publishing

3f FutureTech

 About the activity

Task type	opinion gap
Task outcome	Students share opinions, and agree/disagree.

Introduction

The future of technology doesn't look that promising: there are troubling implications of technology even when it is intended for good purposes. This task asks the students to consider potential new technology in terms of how likely they seem to be, when they may become a reality and their potential positive and negative applications.

Variation, extension, task repetition

- After the task, listen to the accompanying interview. Listen for content: *which invention are they talking about? Do they have similar opinions to you?* Then pick out potential items for language focus.
- Get students to rank the inventions from least useful to most useful, or least likely to most likely, or safest to most dangerous.
- Search for something along the lines of *weird inventions* – then bring some resulting images to class. Alternately, ask the students to google this, and find a picture they can show on their phones to other groups. Students use the pictures in order to use the frame above from the main task (when, how useful, any dangers) to present their invention. They listen to each other's presentations before choosing their favourite.

Language feedback options

- Modals/other forms for predicting the future: *it could become real very soon; there's no chance this will happen, it won't happen for a long time, it seems likely soon.*
- Future perfect: *it will probably have been created by the end of the century*
- The passive: *files can be shared… it can be programmed to…*
- Expressing utility/benefits/drawbacks: *it could be useful for…, it could help people to…, it allows you to…, …lets you + Verb; it seems of limited use as…, there are some possible dangers here, it's worrying because…*
- Making comparisons: *…is far more useful than…, compared to X, it's not very useful*
- Lexis related to technology: *app, tablet, features, bugs AI, the cloud, to program/reprogram, to implant a microchip, to scan,*
- Participle clauses/complex noun phrases: *a robot dog originally designed to act as a soldier*

 **How to run the activity**

Levels	A2–B2
Ages	13+
Length	30 minutes

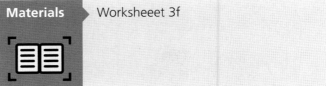

Materials ▸ Worksheeet 3f

Pre-task

- A good starting point for this task would be to show a short video clip illustrating future technology – whether fiction or documentary. Show the clip and ask the students to react to the technology they see: *does it look useful? Can you see any negative consequences? When do you think it will be invented by?*
- If you can't find a clip, use an invention that you think would be of interest to the group e.g. a household AI (see **2b Domestic robot**). Ask the same questions as above.

Main task

- Tell students you will give them a short fact file about an invention. They should note the name of the invention and then do the same as the pre-task, in pairs or small groups i.e. decide:

  a. when it might be invented (if at all!)
  b. how useful it seems
  c. any possible dangers

Ask each group to finish their discussion by agreeing on brief answers for each item e.g. *maybe by 2050; it could be useful for helping at home; no real dangers, but maybe it will take jobs from people.*

- Let each group have 2 or 3 minutes with each fact file. This could either be done as a gallery walk, or they could pass the fact files along from group to group, changing when you give a signal indicating that time is up.
- When all groups have looked at all fact files, conduct some brief feedback on the items.

3f FutureTech – the fact files 1–3

1. The synthetic companion

- A synthetic life-size AI companion, designed to be a friend, partner or just a domestic helper.
- Physical appearance can be tailored in advance via a computer programme.
- Personality can be programmed to make him/her kind, caring, adventurous etc.
- Further in the future, the memories and personality of a loved one may be "uploaded" into its brain.
- Does not need food or medicine, simply needs to be plugged in to recharge for 4 hours per night.

2. The mind's eye

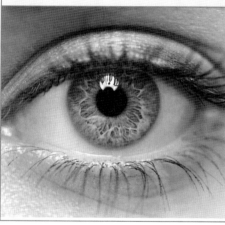

- A small microchip is implanted in the brain of the user.
- This allows the user to *rewind* memories of the day, week or month, to view them again.
- Memories are therefore made more reliable.
- With permission, files can be shared across users i.e. it will be possible to view the memories/experiences of other people.
- Information concerning crimes must be shared with government and police, and can be used in a court of law.

3. Canine soldier

- A robot dog originally designed to act as a soldier.
- Designed to replace human soldiers: there will no longer be human deaths in wars.
- Highly skilled and equipped with a range of tools for disabling enemies.
- Solar-powered and constantly active.
- Can be reprogrammed to be used at home for civilian purposes – a repair dog/guard dog/companion.

© DELTA Publishing, 2019 | www.deltapublishing.co.uk
ISBN 978-3-12-501701-6

ACTIVITIES FOR TASK-BASED LEARNING
by Neil Anderson and Neil McCutcheon

3f FutureTech – the fact files 4–6

Perfect partner finder

- A dating service that promises to find you the perfect romantic partner.
- You spend the night in a clinic, sleeping. While asleep, an AI scans your memories and personality.
- It then matches you with a suitable partner. You go on a simulated date, all while asleep.
- When you wake up, you can arrange to meet in real life.

The child tracker tablet

- For worried parents everywhere, this tablet can tell you where you child is exactly, at any time.
- Through a chip implanted in the child, it can also tell you how they feel, if they are in pain, hot, cold, hungry etc.
- Advanced technology allows you to see what the child is seeing, through their eyes.
- App can be programmed to stop the child from seeing or doing harmful things.

Cloud life paradise

- Amazing technology allows you to transfer your brain/consciousness into a computer – you become part of the cloud.
- You can then have a wide range of adventures or experiences, as if they are really happening.
- Spend months on a paradise beach; climb Everest; look for ancient secrets in the Amazon; become famous; fall in love with the perfect partner. All are possible.
- It can be used on your deathbed, creating a form of eternal life.

ACTIVITIES FOR TASK-BASED LEARNING
by Neil Anderson and Neil McCutcheon

© DELTA Publishing, 2019 | www.deltapublishing.co.uk
ISBN 978-3-12-501701-6

3g Changes

 About the activity

Task type	interview a partner
Task outcome	Students find out who has changed the most over a set time period.

Introduction

"Times change, and we with time" – but is there some essence in each person that remains the same? Students of whatever age will enjoy discussing how they have changed, and even small changes in style, appearance and tastes will be important to any self-absorbed teenagers you teach. As adults, it's interesting to look back over our lives, or as an alternative at the changes that have happened to a place that we are familiar with.

Variations, extension, task repetition

- If you think students would rather talk about how a place has changed, you could begin with some old photographs of the city or town where the school is located or where you grew up. In this context, the passive can arise very naturally: *was built, knocked down, converted into; was intended/supposed to be used as…*

Language feedback operations

- Adjectives to describe personality and appearance; nouns to describe types e.g. *I was shy/a real animal lover/non-conformist/pain in the ***/the life and soul of the party.*
- Words for fashion and hairstyles: *mullet, ponytail, trainers, crop top…*
- Words for youth cults and musical styles: *Goth, grunge*
- *Used to* to talk about changes over time. *Used to* and *would* to talk about habitual behaviour in the past. See also **5a Nostalgia story.**
- *What were you like?* as opposed to *What kind of things did you like?*
- Phrases to talk about preferences: *a film buff, a Queen fan, football crazy, crazy about…, really into …*
- Relative clauses: *I was the kind of person who…*
- The question about an ideal partner can lead to the use of modal auxiliaries to talk about hypotheticals e.g. *I shouldn't have… I would have liked to be with …*

▶ How to run the activity

Levels	A2–C2
Ages	all, especially adults
Length	45 minutes

Materials	Worksheet 3g

Pre-task

- Ask adult students to bring in a photograph of themselves as teenagers. You could also do the same! Tell the students *what you were like* as a teenager: Were you well-behaved or rebellious, sporty, a member of a "gang" or more or a loner? Were you creative in some way? What were your ambitions? (and so on)
- The students should be encouraged to ask you questions at this stage.
- Now exploit their photographs. They could use these as the basis of a "long turn" i.e. where they speak to one or two of their classmates about themselves as teenagers. This can work well with lower levels, as it involves familiar, everyday vocabulary. (This stage will, of course, be more productive if the students have some time to make notes, and this is particularly important at low levels.)
- Steps 1–3 can be done with teenagers, though the photos will be of them in the more recent past – whatever era you feel they will be comfortable with.
- One optional lead-in to this with a more advanced class is to read the opening page of The Catcher In The Rye by J.D. Salinger with some prompt questions to encourage the students to find out about Holden Cauldfield, and to read beyond the surface meaning to speculate about what kind of person he is.
- You will likely want to do some feedback on language that arises to describe character: *rebellious, sensitive,* etc.

Main task

- Either use the worksheet, or brainstorm some ways that people can change over time. You will want to vary the details of the list to suit your student group.
- Regroup the students so that they are working with different people from the ones they worked with on the pre-task. Groups of three work well.
- Their task is to ask as many questions as they need to in order to find out who has changed the most/least, since they were teenagers or over the last ten years. (Although you'll want to try to compare over a similar time period within each group, so that the task is meaningful, stay flexible with respect to the time-frame, as in some cases older students will claim that they have not changed significantly in a decade!)

3g Changes – what were you like?

Who has changed the most?

Ask about...	Student 1	Student 2
appearance (hair)		
appearance (dress)		
personality		
hobbies and interests		
taste in films, music, food		
boyfriends/girlfriends		
an *ideal* partner		
favourite possessions		
political views		
people you admired		

© DELTA Publishing, 2019 | www.deltapublishing.co.uk
ISBN 978-3-12-501701-6

ACTIVITIES FOR TASK-BASED LEARNING
by Neil Anderson and Neil McCutcheon

4 Problem-solving

4a Bad neighbours

 About the activity

Task type	Problem-solving
Task outcome	Students share two sides of a story heard through a jigsaw listening and decide where the truth lies.

Introduction

Most of us live in close proximity to others – whether in an apartment block or a semi-detached house – and yet we do not choose who these others are! Sometimes we get lucky, with neighbours who have similar wishes and lifestyles, but often we don't – our habits and expectations clash. This task exploits the latter in the form of a jigsaw listening: students listen to a story of neighbours who don't get on, hearing it from one of two perspectives. They must share this information in order to make a (subjective) decision as to where the truth lies, and what they – as the landlord – can do about it.

Variations, extension, task repetition

- Bad neighbours are a staple of sitcoms and dramas: if you know a clip of a scene involving neighbourly strife that would appeal to your students, show it to them with a simple task such as *Who is the worse neighbour in this scene and why?*
- You can also use the ideas and language from here or **3d Tenancy agreement** to act out a "mediation" role play following the landlord interviews with Paul and Anthony. Imagine all three parties – Paul, Paul's landlady, Anthony – have come together for a follow-up meeting. In groups of three, students do a role play, each trying to achieve a favourable outcome for themselves.

Language feedback options

- Lexis related to expected *or* anti-social behaviour: *to complain/make a complaint about someone, make (lots of) noise, be nosy/bossy, keep things tidy, behave respectfully/politely, follow the rules.*
- Present simple/continuous for expressing annoying habits: *he's always smoking in the lift, they have parties every weekend.*
- Expressing opinions: (see separate list). *I don't think it's his fault*
  The grammar (and lexis) of reported speech: *He told me that you had gone out and left the front door open… He complained about + Noun Phrase.*
- Lexis related to tenancy and tenancy agreements: *public areas, shared facilities, follow/break rules (of tenancy), building manager, to give someone notice, to evict someone*

How to run the activity

Levels	A2+
Ages	13+
Length	30 minutes

Materials  List of typical complaints from neighbours

Worksheet 4a: Students can use this to take notes while they listen, and then identify discrepancies.

Pre-task

- Give students an example of a problem you had with a neighbour – ideally a real one, but it could be imagined: *we had one neighbour who was so angered by the noise of our washing machine that she tried to make a rule for the whole building that clothes should only be washed on a Saturday afternoon (when she was not at home)* or *Our downstairs neighbour was not happy that we once had a party for our 5-year-old son and his friends. Within 20 minutes of the party, he came up and said they were running around too much – from now on they should only play games or talk while sitting down for the rest of the afternoon.* Ask your students if this seems fair or not – try to elicit their honest opinion (these will hopefully vary).

Task 1 (optional)

- Elicit typical complaints that neighbours make. These could be complaints they have made or received, or just more general ones. Board these. If it is easier, you can add from the list on the worksheet below (grade the language as appropriate); try to end up with between 5–10.
- Ask students to choose five and to rank these problems from *most* to *least* problematic. They should try to agree, but as this can be very subjective, it is not a problem if they cannot agree. Feedback on the ones they thought were most problematic, finding out why they decided this.

Main task

- Introduce the two main characters of the story: Paul is a student who lives with his flatmates above Anthony, a retired teacher. Ideally, find and use appropriate pictures to bring them to life: be careful not to caricature either character, as you want the students to listen to the story in a reasonably unbiased way. Paul has lived in a rented flat for about 6 months; Anthony owns his and has lived there for 20 years. They have not really communicated before but there have been problems on both sides. The situation has come to a head, and the landlady (the students) must listen to both sides of the story, identify the truth, and offer suggestions.
- Tell the students they will act as the landlady, listening to one version of events, before coming together, hearing the other version, and trying to decide a) what seems to be true/false b) what advice they can give to solve the situation.
- Divide the class into two groups of equal size: Group A will listen to Paul, and Group B will listen to Anthony. They can download the recording from the DELTA Augmented app, and use headphones if necessary. Remind them that they will be sharing what they heard with the other group at the end.
- When they are ready, ask them to play their version of the story. They should take notes of the complaints made including details given of what happened. It may be easier for your students to listen once for gist – *identify the complaints* – and then a second time for detail – *take notes of some of the details of the complaint*. Monitor the two groups and encourage them to take control of the audio equipment, replaying anything they did not hear clearly. Allow 10–15 minutes for this phase.

- Now regroup the students so members of each group (Group A and Group B) come together: they can work in pairs, AB, or groups of four, ABAB, depending on the size of the group and the abilities of the students. They should discuss what they heard, going through each complaint and the details surrounding it; their task is to find discrepancies between the stories. They will then use this to form and agree on an evaluation of the situation: *is one of the tellers more reliable? Who do you believe and why?*
- As a class, students should now give their views: allow them to debate and disagree concerning who is more reliable – this may be based on both what they heard and their own experience and prejudices.
- Finally, in small groups, they decide what realistic action they can/should take in order to resolve the situation; see the ideas to the right, and of course allow the students to add any other ideas they have.

Typical complaints from neighbours

- Late-night parties
- Noise through the floor/walls
- Mess/disturbance from pets
- Noisy children
- Smoking/drinking in public areas
- Responsibility for tidiness and upkeep of public areas
- Use of shared facilities (parking, laundry)
- Health and safety issues e.g. hygiene, rubbish

What to do?

- Make a complaint about Anthony to the building managers.
- Do nothing.
- Give Paul new rules and conditions.
- Give Paul notice, telling him to leave the flat.

© DELTA Publishing, 2019 | www.deltapublishing.co.uk
ISBN 978-3-12-501701-6

ACTIVITIES FOR TASK-BASED LEARNING
by Neil Anderson and Neil McCutcheon

4a Bad neighbours – what they said

What Paul said	What Anthony said	Differences?

.... (fold here) ....

Suggested answers:

What Anthony said	What Paul said
He doesn't wear shoes indoors. (His family follows the rules.)	Every day Anthony's family walk up and down in their boots making noise.
He was patient when explaining this to Paul.	Anthony was angry with him and got red in the face.
He doesn't like the smell of Paul's cooking: perhaps fish or liver?	He's a vegetarian – he says vegetables, and sometimes chicken.
Paul's dog is noisy and it left dog mess outside his door.	"Why would my puppy do that?" Anthony can't prove that Sally left dog mess
He only puts out one bag of rubbish every three days.	Anthony puts out a new rubbish bag every day so there is no room for Paul's bags.
He doesn't like football and he wasn't making a noise during the England v Albania match. (It was the neighbours above them making the noise.)	Anthony and his friends were like hooligans and threw glass bottles out of the window when England lost the match.
Paul's friends stand on their balcony talking loudly.	He doesn't make noise. Just once last week he had a reunion with colleagues. It's an exception to the rule.

© DELTA Publishing, 2019 | www.deltapublishing.co.uk
ISBN 978-3-12-501701-6

ACTIVITIES FOR TASK-BASED LEARNING
by Neil Anderson and Neil McCutcheon

4b Fake News!

 About the activity

Task type	Problem-solving
Task outcome	Students agree on which story is not true, and why, before checking this online.

Introduction

The current use of the term "fake news" can be traced back to 2016, when there was a surge of news stories on social media related to the US election: these were later established to be entirely false. The phenomenon is of course much older – as long as they have told stories, people have shown a remarkable ability to be creative with the truth, whether gently embellishing existing events or outright fabricating them. This task involves learners reading and summarising surprising or incredible stories to each other, before trying to agree on which one/ones seem to be false and, for the true stories, deciding which details have been misreported or exaggerated.

Variation, extension, task repetition

Ideally, if possible, conduct feedback on the main task by asking the learners to find out for themselves by searching for key names from the stories online. They should soon verify that *The (Un)Luckiest Man Alive* is not true but the other three are. Ask learners to look again at the true stories, comparing them to the online source they found. Are there any facts that are different from the version they found online? Can they find extra facts/details online that were not in the version they read and listened to in class? Be prepared to summarise these to the others.

Language feedback options

- Decide based on which words may need to be pre-taught from each text.
- After the main task feedback/extension, they can mine their texts for further phrases/structures that seem important. See the suggestions on text-mining in the introduction.
- The main task step 2 is a great opportunity for learners to use language to speculate, assert and give views and reasons (see below). You could either let them speculate about one of the texts, and then feed in some language for doing so, before they continue; or simply pay attention to the forms they use across the stage, then working with recasting/reformulating this after main task step 3.
    a. Expressing scepticism: *there's no way X can be true as…, it's (just) not realistic/plausible, it doesn't make sense, it seems strange/made-up/implausible, X/that couldn't happen, it's not possible for (people) to…*
    b. Expressing certainty: *I know this one is true, I've heard it before, I think it's absolutely possible for…*
    c. Being somewhere in the middle: *I guess it could be true, there's some truth in it, it sounds familiar, but I'm not sure, some parts seem plausible. For instance, the bit where…*
    d. Giving reasons: *it can't be true as…, it's (highly) improbable that…, it can't be true for the following reasons…*

▶ **How to run the activity**

Levels	B1+
Ages	13+
Length	30 minutes

Materials	Worksheet 4b

Pre-task

- Board the titles for the four stories: *The Girl Who Fell from the Sky; The Dog who would not leave his Master; The (Un)Luckiest Man Alive; The Men, The Tree, The Croc* (check learners know what this last word stands for i.e. crocodile). Tell the learners that these are all very surprising stories – unbelievable stories, except that they are true … mostly. One of them is invented, and the others can be found in some form on the internet. Ask students in small groups to make some guesses as to what each story could be about.

Task 1

- Divide the class into four groups and give out one story to each student, so that an equal number of stories have been given out. Ask the students to read their story. Their task is to comment on the following:
  a) Do they believe it is true? Why, why not?
  b) Are there any details in the story that might not be real e.g. might be exaggerated through re-telling?
  They should then read the story alone before sharing their opinion with a partner who read the same text.
- Allow students a chance to check three or four words/phrases in their text that they feel are very important to know for the main task. They should work them out together from the context, with guidance from the teacher. Do stress that they don't need to understand everything at this point.

Main task

- Working with someone who has read the same story, they should extract some of the key information/key words from the story: their goal is to re-tell it without looking at the text, giving enough information for the listener to decide whether it is true or not. They should write the key words on a piece of paper.
- Regroup the students so they are in a group with all the texts present. Ask them to take turns to tell their story using the key words. The listeners should decide whether they think it is a true story or fake news, giving reasons why.
- For feedback, you can let the students know the real answer: *The (Un)Luckiest Man Alive* is the example of fake news here as it is entirely made-up. It could be the learners knew this as they have heard of the other stories: Hachiko, for instance, is quite well known. See the extension ideas, however, for further possible work: not all the facts in each story are true, with some information differing from that which you can find online.

4b Fake News! – stories 1 + 2

Story 1: the girl who fell from the sky

Juliana Koepcke was a 14-year-old German girl living in the city of Pullcapa, Peru with her parents, who were researchers in the Amazonian jungle. In 1971 she took a flight with her mother, returning her to school in Lima. Not long into the flight, the plane flew into a huge, terrible storm, which shook the plane so violently that it fell apart in the sky. Juliana, still strapped in her seat, fell 3000 metres down into the jungle below. She woke up several hours later, and was, amazingly, only slightly injured: she had survived the fall, protected by her seat. Sadly, though, she was the only survivor: her mother and all of the other 100 passengers had died in the crash. She was now alone and lost, deep in the Amazonian jungle. She calmly remembered some of the lessons her father had taught her: for instance, if you are in the jungle, you should travel downhill, as you will find water; and you should then follow that water downstream in order to escape the jungle. She did this, following a stream for more than 10 days. It was difficult: she had water but no food, and insects bit her and laid their eggs in her arms. After walking for more than two weeks, she found a small house by the river, where she rested and waited for someone to return. While she waited, she poured gas on her arms to help with the insect bites; this worked, as more than 50 small worms crawled out of the wounds. Finally, some fishermen arrived and took care of her, sailing her down the river in a 7-hour journey to the largest local town. From there, she was flown to her father in Pullcapa. She survived, and later became a biologist like her parents.

Story 2: the dog who would not leave his master

"Chuken Hachiko" – in English, faithful Hachiko – is a symbol of loyalty in Japan and beyond; particularly the loyalty of a dog to their master. Hidesaburo Ueno, Hachiko's master, was a professor at Tokyo University who travelled every day by train to his workplace. Everyday Hachiko left the house in the morning with his master, returned home once he was on the train, and then left again in the afternoon, travelling to the station in order to meet his master when he returned home from work. But one day, in 1925, Ueno never returned from his workplace: sadly, he had died from a heart attack at his workplace. Hachiko arrived at the station at the usual time – just when his master's train arrived. But, of course, Ueno was not on the train. Why is this story special? Because Hachiko, for the next ten years, continued to travel to the station on his own in the morning. He'd wait all day for his master to arrive, sitting outside the station until his master's old train arrived back from his workplace. Local people began to notice the dog, and, feeling sorry for him, started to feed him while he waited; eventually, in 1932, national newspapers picked up the story and his fame spread across Japan. Hachiko died in 1936. As his story became known, parents told their children about him as a lesson in faithfulness; statues were made to remember him; the station entrance was named after him; eventually, films in both Japanese and English were made about this famously loyal dog.

ACTIVITIES FOR TASK-BASED LEARNING
by Neil Anderson and Neil McCutcheon
© DELTA Publishing, 2019 | www.deltapublishing.co.uk
ISBN 978-3-12-501701-6

4b Fake News! – stories 3 + 4

Story 3: The (un)luckiest man alive

They say that lightning never strikes the same place twice: try telling this to Alberto Sanchez, a Cuban man who has been struck by lightning twice in his life. The first was as a teenager, when he was caught in a storm while playing football, and was not quick enough to follow the team to shelter. The second time was later in his life when he was working with a friend on building an extension to his house – after a storm started, he ran outside to carry some of the tools they had been using back inside. Both times, incredibly, he suffered minor injuries and spent only a few hours in hospital. Being struck twice by lightning is remarkable enough, but this is far from the only accident Sanchez has experienced and survived: as a child he was in a car accident when a speeding car hit the one his parents were driving, forcing them off the road. The car was badly damaged, but all those inside survived. In his early twenties, he went on a boat trip with university friends when a terrible storm came out of nowhere; after trying to sail the board back to land, a huge wave hit it, capsizing the vessel and throwing those on board into the water. Sanchez, who was wearing a life jacket, survived, though two others drowned. But the event Sanchez says was the most frightening was caused by man not nature: in his early thirties, he was caught up in a bank robbery. The robbers failed to escape the bank before the police arrived, and so they took two customers hostage, one of whom was (of course!) Sanchez. After keeping him at gunpoint in the bank for four hours, they escaped with him in their getaway car, which the police eventually managed to stop, arresting the robbers. Sanchez was unhurt. Is he the unluckiest man alive or the luckiest? "I think, overall," says Sanchez, "I have much to thank God for."

Story 4: The men, the tree, the croc

The Northern Territory is Australia's least populated region, despite being over a million square kilometres in area. However, man shares this vast area with numerous other species, not least of which is the saltwater crocodile, which thrives in the coastal river systems. There have been many tragic encounters between man and croc. One such happened in 2000, in the Finniss River, about 100 kms from the capital city Darwin. Three friends had been enjoying a day of quad biking near the river and were covered in mud; they decided to clean off in the river. While doing so, the friends suddenly saw a six-metre saltwater crocodile, but before they could escape, it snatched one of them and pulled him underwater. The other two hurried to a tree on the bank of the river, climbing up it for safety. They looked anxiously for any sign of their friend – there had been no noise, no struggle; he had simply disappeared under the water with the crocodile. After some time, the animal surfaced, bringing the dead body of their friend with him: they knew for sure now that, tragically, their friend had been killed by the creature. The crocodile disappeared again but some time later reappeared in the water below the tree, watching and waiting. The friends were stuck up the tree for more than two days while the crocodile waited for them to come down; all this time, they tried to keep each other awake to stop them from falling out of the tree while sleeping. Eventually, worried family members contacted the police, and a search helicopter was sent out to look for them: it found them in the tree, and after some time lifted them to safety. The crocodile was hunted and shot a week or two later, but the body of the friend was, sadly, never found.

© DELTA Publishing, 2019 | www.deltapublishing.co.uk
ISBN 978-3-12-501701-6

ACTIVITIES FOR TASK-BASED LEARNING
by Neil Anderson and Neil McCutcheon

4c Pictures and lies

 About the activity

Task type	Problem-solving / information gap
Task outcome	Students collaborate to decide which one of four peers they are interviewing does not really have a picture and is in fact inventing their description.

Introduction

This task is based on one that we learned from our colleague, Steve Oakes. We like it because of its flexibility: the pictures can be selected based on the theme of the rest of the lesson. As with many of our tasks, it can function as one task in a sequence (e.g. a lead-in to planning a day out).

Variation, extension, task repetition

- As well as the theme, you can play with the number of pictures and therefore group sizes, depending on the size of your class. It's even possible for one-to-one lessons: ask your student to bring in two or three photos and to describe four – you decide which one is not real. Then reverse the roles.
- After language focus, you can repeat the task in these ways:
  - let students in threes study the pictures for a minute or two (so you need multiple copies at this stage). Give each student one of the pictures, hidden from the view of the other group members. They then describe it to their partners but invent some details. The others listen and try to identify what the false information is based on their memory of the picture.
  - Have learners find a new picture related to the theme, using their phones in class (or finding one for homework). They mingle and describe, with the task of finding their "favourite" description / picture based on what they hear. Or describe and draw: in pairs the students take turn to describe their picture with the partner listening and drawing what they hear. They then compare.

Language feedback options

- A variety of question forms (see the table above; note that this can be restricted further depending on level and can even be limited to *is there / are there…?*).
- Describing a scene: a) present continuous: *they are having a picnic, some children are swimming in the sea, the sun is shining* b) *There is / there are: there is a family by a tree.*
- Relative and participle clauses: *There is a family (who are) sitting under an umbrella; a girl wearing pink is on the sand.*
- Adjectives to describe the people and objects in the picture: *a tall man, a little boy, grey cloudy sky, a beautiful day.*
- Prepositional phrases: *next to the stage, in front of the family, by the pool.*
- Topic-related lexis based on the pictures selected.

> **Sample questions to support Group 2:**
> *How many (people / animals / trees etc) are there?*
> *Are they outside or inside?*
> *What is the weather like?*
> *What time of day is it?*
> *What are the people doing?*
> *How do they feel?*

How to run the activity

Levels	A1–B1		**Materials**	Worksheet 4c: You can use the pictures here or bring your own to class. This is just an example. If you choose a different topic, you will need to bring different pictures.
Ages	8 – adult			
Length	15–30 minutes			Four envelopes.

Pre-task

- Ask for four volunteers (**Group 1**) and move them to one side of the classroom, and the rest of the class (**Group 2**) to the other side: sufficiently apart so they cannot hear each other very well in during the subsequent preparation stages. Instruct the whole class at once (as both groups need to understand what the goal of the other is): **Group 1** will be given one picture each, connected to the theme of the day *A Fun Day Out*. But – a single member of **Group 1** doesn't really have a picture (it can help here if you physically demonstrate the fact some envelopes have a picture and one is empty). **Group 2** should find out which one doesn't really have a picture. They will do this by interviewing all of **Group 1** one by one and then reaching a decision.

- They now need to prepare, and you will have to multi-task here, moving between groups.

- **Group 1** should now each open their envelope. If they have a picture (**ABC** in the worksheet), they should remember as much information/detail as they can before they are interviewed. If they don't have a picture (**D** in the worksheet), they should imagine *A Fun Day Out* scene using the prompts on card **D.** Tip: it helps to pre-select a more confident and creative student for the role of **D.**

- **Group 2** should brainstorm questions to ask about a picture showing *A Fun Day Out.* Ask them to think of questions about people, activities, scenery, weather etc. If it helps, give some prompts (see the box to the right).

Main task

- Group the students so that each one with a picture is now interviewed by two (or more) learners from **Group 2**. Let them start, reminding **Group 2** they need to identify who does not have a picture. They then interview the individual about the picture, trying to find out as much as they can about it.

- When time is up, rotate the four members of **Group 1** so they have new interviewers. Then repeat this process until everyone in **Group 2** has had a chance to interview everyone in **Group 1.** So, based on this version, there should be four rotations.

- Conduct feedback: have **Group 1** line up at the front of the class. Ask the others to say who did not have a picture and why they believe some but not others. Allow for debate and discussion if it is forthcoming. Then ask **Group 1** to open their envelope and slowly reveal their picture…or lack thereof, thereby showing who in fact was the creative member of **Group 1**. If anyone in **Group 2** is surprised/was wrong in their guess, discuss this further e.g. *why did you think they had a picture?*

4c Pictures and lies: a fun day out – the pictures

1

2

3

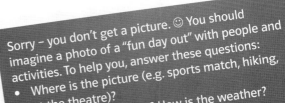

Sorry – you don't get a picture. ☺ You should imagine a photo of a "fun day out" with people and activities. To help you, answer these questions:
- Where is the picture (e.g. sports match, hiking, at the theatre)?
- What time of day is it? How is the weather?
- How many people can you see? What clothes are they wearing and why?
- Do they seem happy? Why?
- Are the people families, friends or strangers?
- What is happening? What activities (e.g. watching and playing sport, eating drinking, talking, reading, relaxing)?

4

ACTIVITIES FOR TASK-BASED LEARNING
by Neil Anderson and Neil McCutcheon

© DELTA Publishing, 2019 | www.deltapublishing.co.uk
ISBN 978-3-12-501701-6

DELTA Publishing

4d Identity swap

 About the activity

Task type	question and answer
Task outcome	Students find out how well they know other members of the class.

Introduction

This is another classic technique for creating an information gap, and which is preparation-light. Students have to imagine that they are another member of the class, and answer questions as they think that person would. The questions can be specially prepared for this activity, or they can be any set of personalised questions from the coursebook you are using. If the class has been together for some time, you can use the activity as a way of cementing bonds within the group, or for reflecting on their time together at the end of the year.

Language feedback opportunities

- Language to talk about similarities and differences: *Me too, Both of us, Neither of us, I do but you don't.*
- Talking about preferences: *I love / like / enjoy / hate / can't stand X… she doesn't mind talking about her feelings*
- The grammar and sequence of tenses for reporting speech: *I thought/put down that you were… You once told me that you liked… I forgot/remembered that you…*
- Reporting predictions: *I got that (one) right/wrong, I could tell that you were…*
- Idioms and expressions: *easy to get to know, a private person, he plays his cards close to his chest, she keeps her own counsel*

Example questions: art

Do you often go to art galleries?
What is a particular period or style of art that appeals to you?
What kind of pictures do you have on the walls at home?
How do you feel about modern art?
Have you ever painted or taken photographs as a hobby?

Example questions: shopping A2

Do you like shopping?
How often do you go shopping for food/clothes – and for fun?
Do you buy a lot of things online?
You recently spent a lot of money on ....
You usually do your Christmas shopping weeks before/a few days before Christmas.

 © DELTA Publishing, 2019 | www.deltapublishing.co.uk
ISBN 978-3-12-501701-6

ACTIVITIES FOR TASK-BASED LEARNING
by Neil Anderson and Neil McCutcheon

How to run the activity

Levels	A2 +
Ages	all
Length	30 minutes

Materials	A short questionnaire: You can find two examples here.

Pre-task

- To lead in to the activity, ask how well the students know each other. (If it's a new class, you can put a different spin on this by asking whether you can learn a lot of people just from the way they look and dress.)
- Divide the class into pairs. These could be students who work together a lot, but if you want the pairs to be random, students can choose picture halves from a hat, then find their new partner.
- Give out a series of questions, such as in the examples below. Tell the students that they must answer these just as they expect their partner would. Allow time for them to complete this preparation stage.

Main task

- Students now compare with their partner to find out how good their guesses were. They can be encouraged to reflect on reasons for their right/wrong answers.
- Pairs report back on how well they did know each other in the end.

Example questions: money and shopping B1 +

Are you good with money, or just good at spending it?
Do you budget every month?
What is something that you bought recently that you think is extravagant?
Have you ever bought something that you then thought was a waste of money?
What's a little luxury that you can't resist?

Example questions: relationships

Do you remember your friends'/partner's birthday?
Are you tidier or messier than your friend/partner/flatmate?
Do you do an equal share of the housework, or more/less than this?
When you have arguments at home, who starts them? Who helps to solve them?
Do you need to spend some time alone?

ACTIVITIES FOR TASK-BASED LEARNING
by Neil Anderson and Neil McCutcheon

© DELTA Publishing, 2019 | www.deltapublishing.co.uk
ISBN 978-3-12-501701-6

5 Sharing experiences

5a Nostalgia story

 About the activity

Task type	anecdote
Task outcome	Students recall and share experiences related to events and time periods we feel nostalgic about.

Introduction

Nostalgia originally referred to an illness: specifically, the acute pain of homesickness. Thankfully, it now tends to be associated with a more positive, albeit wistful, recall of happy experiences located at some point in the past. We tend to feel nostalgic and express our nostalgia rather frequently. This task encourages learners to engage in this: they both recall and recite past experiences, but also listen actively to their partners doing the same, meaning this task is one part monologue, one part dialogue.

Variation, extension, task repetition

- The procedure on the next page suggests eliciting a range of topics, but this can be narrowed as seems appropriate to your class.
- If learners are at the lower end of the suggested band, you will need to make some changes. For instance, it is likely that they may have some familiarity with the past simple, but little with *used to/would*; in this case, the teacher model and language focus should concentrate only on *used to* in contrast to past simple.
- For the Language Focus after the task, ask the students to look back at their key words and reflect on the grammar they used when they first told the story. Ask: *did you just use the past simple? Could you use used to/would at certain points? Where?* Give them a minute or two to decide where they could "upgrade" the forms they used.

Tell them they are going to tell their story again, but this time with a new partner. Regroup the class so all students have a new partner. They then repeat steps 2–5 from the original task.

Language feedback options

Tell the learners you now intend to share a time you feel nostalgic about. They should listen, and with their partner, decide on a follow-up question to ask.
- Tell your story, and have the learners ask further questions.
- Give students a transcript of your story. Ask the learners to look through and identify different verb forms used for the past.
- Focus the learners on sentences you used in your story that reveal different structures for past habit. E.g.: *I used to travel to the seaside every year in July, we'd spend the day swimming in the sea, we often visited our friends, as they stayed nearby.*
- Focus learners on the rules of use/form of the structures; revise what they know and help them understand the precise rules for new structures (e.g. past simple for past habits, states and single events; *used to* for past habits and states; *would* for past habits but not states).

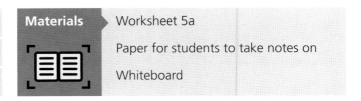

▶ How to run the activity

Levels	A2 – B2
Ages	adults
Length	30 + minutes

Materials	Worksheet 5a
	Paper for students to take notes on
	Whiteboard

Pre-task

- Elicit *nostalgia* and the chunks *to feel nostalgic about / to reminisce about…* from the learners.
- Brainstorm topics we typically feel nostalgic about onto the whiteboard. This is likely to be topics such as *holidays when we were younger, school/university, friends from the past, Xmas and other celebrations, places we lived, pets, hobbies we had.*
- Tell the learners that everyone is going to recall a topic they feel nostalgic about. Ask each learner to choose a topic from the list – one that they have happy memories about and are happy to share with the others in the class.
- Explain that they are going to share their experiences, but before doing so, you want them to note some key words to help them share. They should write a vertical list of 10–15 key words and phrases which they can refer to when sharing their nostalgia story e.g. *summer holidays, go to the beach, swim in the sea, have barbecues, visit friends' summer houses* etc.
- Let the students have 5 minutes or so to note their key words.

Task

- When they have finished taking notes, ask the students to work in pairs of A and B.
- A first tells their story; B should listen and think of questions to ask, for extra information. This can be as natural while A is talking; or, if preferred, at the end when A has finished recalling the nostalgia story.
- This is then repeated, with B telling their story and A asking questions.
- Allow each student about 5 minutes to tell their story and answer questions.
- Ask each student to report back (either to the class, or to a new partner) on the content of their partner's story: anything they had in common; something particularly interesting etc. Share what you heard while monitoring and ask follow-up questions yourself.

5a Nostalgia story

A:

Key words and phrases for my story	Which language could I use from the teacher's story?

-------------------------------- (fold here) --------------------------------

B:

Look at the script of the teacher's story and answer these questions:

- **What verb forms are used?**
- **Are there any forms you didn't use?**
- **Could you use some of these? Add them to the table in A.**

I'd say my happiest memories come from when I lived in Japan. I lived there in the 1980s, when I was a young boy, and overall I think it was the happiest part of my childhood.

We used to live in a city called Kobe, a seaport and one of the most cosmopolitan cites in the whole country. I remember that every morning we'd travel to school by bus, all the way across town; even though we were just five or six years old, we'd go all the way on our own, which seems crazy now. But it was just so safe, and so stress-free.

We used to have a lot of free time after school, so we'd typically go somewhere to play and maybe even cause trouble. We'd visit the park next to the local shrine, for instance, and we'd play baseball or chase pigeons.

Sometimes, we'd head into the hills to look for wild boar. I remember one time, when we went up there, my friend and I came across a female wild boar and her little piglets. She immediately went on the attack, chasing us out of the forest. I can laugh now, but it was pretty terrifying at the time.

© DELTA Publishing, 2019 | www.deltapublishing.co.uk
ISBN 978-3-12-501701-6
ACTIVITIES FOR TASK-BASED LEARNING
by Neil Anderson and Neil McCutcheon

5b Talking about a song

 About the activity

Task type	mini-presentation
Task outcome	Students describe the meaning of the lyrics of a song and say why the song is important to them.

Introduction

Could you live without music? It's common to hear people talk about the "soundtrack of their lives". Sometimes a song stays with us because of where we first heard it, who we were with, or just the combined effect of the melody and lyrics. Or it could be something simpler, like a guitar note or the vocal line or just the beat. In this task, the students have to prepare a mini-presentation on a topic which is likely to be of some interest to them. (See variations below for students who are not interested in music!)
The idea for this task was suggested by a colleague Chris Meoli.

Variation, extension, task repetition

Lower levels might not be able to comment in depth on the lyrics, so they can be encouraged to talk about where and when they first heard the song, and why it's important to them.
• Alternatively, they could talk about a favourite game, film or book.
• Framing the task as a (favourite) song/book/film generally works better than asking for students' all-time favourite.
• For an extension task, ask students to co-operate in groups to create a playlist for a party. (Specify who will be coming to the party – members of the class, or a different group of people?)

Language feedback options

For songs, adjectives and other expressions to talk about music and trends will arise: *melancholy, moving, irresistible, catchy, ground-breaking, innovative, influenced by…, debut, follow-up, the latest release by…*
Asking students to talk about where/when they first heard the song will generate language such as the past simple and continuous tense, *remember + ing, reminds me of + ing, makes me think of + N.*
Search the teacher's model for interesting language. Examples of lexis from my text are the adverb and adjective combinations:

intensely personal *highly original*	*sense of disorientation/* *freedom*	single words *combines* *captures*
collocations and expressions	*complements* .... *perfectly*	*otherworldly* *affecting*

How to run the activity

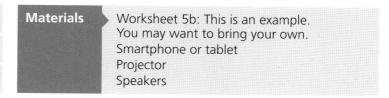

Levels	B1–B2 +
Ages	teens or adults
Length	variable

Materials	Worksheet 5b: This is an example. You may want to bring your own. Smartphone or tablet Projector Speakers

Pre-task

- To lead in to the topic, you could use a musical stimulus to get students to discuss their own interests in music. Sometimes, I have used a "magic square" on which students write the answers to dictated questions, such as:
  - Name one genre or style of music which you enjoy.
  - Name an artist/composer/performer that you admire.
  - What is one song (or album) that you would recommend?
  - Are there any styles of music you *don't* enjoy listening to?
- Now briefly introduce the task and tell the students that you are going to do it first.
- Why not play the song and let students read the lyric at this point. It's good practice to set a "gist" task here. What do they think it is about?
- After students respond briefly in pairs, give your model. Ask students to focus on these questions: *Do they learn anything new about it? Do they want to ask any questions at this stage?*
- There is an example commentary on *Strawberry Fields Forever* by the Beatles below for B2+. Such a model could be simplified or made more elaborate, depending on your students' level and interests. You could provide a written version or, if giving your presentation orally, you may wish to record this on a smartphone. If it is unscripted, this allows you to focus at a later point on language that you have used naturally.

Task

- **Individual stage:** Instruct task. The students have to prepare a similar mini-presentation. The structure of this is up to you, but it should follow your initial model. You should give an approximate time-limit and say whether the presentations should be supported by a visual element. The task works best if you get students to choose a song where the lyrics actually *say* something, but where the meaning *isn't immediately obvious*.
- **Group / class stage:** This is where the students give their short presentations. Depending on the amount of time available, you can do this in groups or as a class. You may wish to share the time out over several lessons, for instance as a timetabled daily event as part of longer classes. It is good to set an audience task, for example to ask questions of the presenter. Other strategies are more risky, such as getting students to vote for the song they would most like to hear.

5b Talking about a song – the model and the notes

This song was written during a phase in the Beatles' live career when they had finished touring and John Lennon was questioning whether they could continue or not. The song is intensely personal and it expresses John Lennon's sense of disorientation following his experiments with psychedelic drugs. Unlike a lot of songs from the same period, which take us into the realms of outer space or fantasy, John's lyrics take the listener back to his childhood. The scene is the Strawberry Fields reform school, which was very near the place where he grew up in Liverpool. The lyric combines two themes – John's isolation and uncertainty about his own identity, and the joy of exploring his imagination into which he beckons the listener to follow. Some of the lines make him appear confused and lonely, like one of the orphans in the school, rebelling against being in the institution – just what Lennon himself was doing at the time. At the same time, the main refrain "nothing to get hung about" captures a sense of freedom and happiness.

After a lot of attempts, and helped by their producer George Martin, the Beatles created a track of otherworldly dream-like music out of two separate recordings, one made with electronic instruments and one with a full orchestra. This complements the lyric perfectly. Martin later described this as "a complete tone poem – like a modern Debussy." There is no doubt that it is highly original and affecting. I remember the first time I heard it as a 12-year-old. My father owned the single but had only ever played the other side. I immediately felt that this music let me into a world that was too strange for my parents to really "get", but one which I intuitively understood.

Presentation preparation prompts

The song I want to tell you about is...

I chose it because ...

The band ...

The song ...

They lyrics are really interesting because...

They make me feel...

I really think you should listen to it because...

ACTIVITIES FOR TASK-BASED LEARNING
by Neil Anderson and Neil McCutcheon

© DELTA Publishing, 2019 | www.deltapublishing.co.uk
ISBN 978-3-12-501701-6

5c Where were you when...?

 About the activity

Task type	personal information gap/short anecdote
Task outcome	Students share where they were and what they were doing at some key moments in history.

Introduction

There are some moments in history that are so sudden, momentous or unexpected that we remember vividly where we were when these events occurred. This task exploits these "frozen moments" to help students create short anecdotes. The moments you choose will depend on the age of students. The most famous ones from the previous generation are the assassination of President Kennedy and the Cuban Missile Crisis. We also offer some other suggestions of events you could choose.

Variation, extension, task repetition

- For a group of students who do not have personal memories attached to broader events, an alternative task is to get them to draw a timeline of their lives with some key dates plotted. They can include when they changed school; moved house, country or job; got married; when their children were born – anything that seems appropriate.

- Now, students swap timelines so that they only have their partner's dates. They now ask some questions about each date to get more information. This information can later be used to write a short biography, with the second student acting as a "ghostwriter" for their interviewee. These biographical summaries can be displayed, and other students can guess the identity of the person based on the information the texts contain.

Language feedback options

This task can be a "focused task" for lower levels – that is, it invites the use of the past continuous tense in contrast with the past simple: *I was living in… working as… I had just got in from school when I heard…*

▶ How to run the activity

Levels	A2 +
Ages	adults
Length	20 minutes

Materials	Worksheet 5c

Pre-task

- Display the key dates around the classroom, and ask if students know what happened on these dates. Allow them to speculate. Some suggested dates are:

  > the murder of John Lennon on 8th December 1980
  > the "Fall" of the Berlin Wall on 9th November 1989
  > the death of Kurt Cobain on 5th April 1994
  > the death of Princess Diana on 31st August 1997
  > the attack on America on 11th September 2001
  > Michael Jackson's death on 25th June 2009
  > David Bowie's death on 10th January 2016

- Find and display pictures of the events so students can match them up. Elicit feedback; respond briefly to anything students say but without asking too many questions at this point.

Main task

- Choose an appropriate date (or dates) for the students in your class – one that most of them remember – or allow them a free choice. The dates needn't be any of the ones above, of course, but something appropriate to students' own culture and age. Explain the task, "Where were you when…?" Students will tend to remember best the times when they were young and going through rapid changes.
- Students complete key details on the worksheet below, which is designed to help them jog their memories. We have found from experience that some people have more vivid memories than others when confronted with such a task.
- For students who do not connect personally with one of these world events, they can choose an event that has particular significance in their personal lives, such as an important "first". The first day in a new school or job can work well. (The death of someone close to them is something else that might occur in this context, but bear in mind that students may not want to talk about this, especially if they do not know the other members of the class well.) Some people remember certain film or music releases quite vividly.
- Encourage students to share their short anecdotes in groups; listeners can ask questions in order to elicit more information, or just react naturally. Alternatively, this can be run as a mingling activity.

5c Where were you when...?

Do you remember where you were at certain moments in history? Talk about the three here and add one of your own.

the 2001 attacks in the USA

the fall of the Berlin Wall

the assassination of John Lennon

Prepare to talk about one key event . Make notes about:

Key event:

- what my life was like at the time (school, college or work)

- who I was with at the time I heard

- where I was when I heard

- how I felt

- "personal aftermath" on that day or in subsequent days

- what this event means to me now

ACTIVITIES FOR TASK-BASED LEARNING
by Neil Anderson and Neil McCutcheon

5d My life in apps

 About the activity

Task type	personalised information gap (show and tell)
Task outcome	Students share their favourite apps, and guess the identities of other students based on their choices. (In option 2, students ask and answer questions about apps they like.)

Introduction

This activity makes use of students' phones and mobile devices, which they usually have readily to hand. Ideally, students actually use their phones to find and share information about the applications, and as a basis for sharing personal information. (The activity can be varied to include computer apps.) As so much of our lives is filled with screen-time, this fits well with the idea of helping students say what they want to say – in English.

Variation, extension, task repetition

- Students can design a new application, including its logo, and describe its features. In "buzz groups" they present these and others, who are IT design consultants, suggest potential problems and improvements. Students, now back with their original groups, discuss which of the suggested upgrades to add. The improved apps can be taken to another stage in a kind of "pyramid discussion", where the best are selected for sharing with the whole class.
- Choose an app for your classmate – based on what students know of their classmates already, or on draft profiles. Each student is given the name/profile of a classmate, and they are tasked with finding at least one app in the app store that would suit this person. If you pair students off at the initial stage, then they can report back, describing their selection to their partner.
- See **3e This house believes...** for another task about social media.

Language feedback options

- Various tech-related vocabulary: *upload, share, edit, copy link, post, comment, personalise, scroll up/down, options, news feed…*
- Infinitive of purpose and related expressions to express causal connections: *This is to upload music, this is for sharing content, This helps with reducing the file size, This lets you/allows you to edit, This is so that other people can access your posts.*
- Conditionals (zero) and related structures: *When you open this window, you get a range of options.*
- Relative and participle clauses: *You see all the posts (that are) tagged with the same tag.*

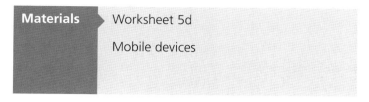

How to run the activity

Levels	B1 +
Ages	teens, young adult, adult
Length	40–60 minutes*

Materials	Worksheet 5d
	Mobile devices

*Option 2 can take at least twice this time

Pre-task

- Depending on the age of your students, you might want to display some screen icons for some very common apps (Facebook, Twitter, Instagram, YouTube) and ask students to identify the apps, and say what they are used for. Obviously, "digital natives" won't need to do this, so an alternative would be to get them to discuss these apps in general. Other triggers for discussion include:
  - "Everyone's on Facebook these days – aren't they?" Do you know anyone who isn't – why not?
  - "My phone told me last week that my daily average screen time was 1 hour and 27 minutes." How do you think I felt? What do you think your average is and how do you feel about this?
  - Ranking the apps on display.
- Collect ideas in feedback, including *features* and *bugs* – focusing especially on the positive qualities of these apps. Try not to let the discussion wander too far at this stage into talking about students' favourite apps, because you don't want to pre-empt the main activity.
- It's a good to model the task (option 1 or 2) now, so that students have an idea of what they are about to do. This will help them know what to look for in the preparatory stages.

Task: Option 1 (See worksheet):

- Each student completes the worksheet with 6 apps that they find useful, or represent who they are. Ideally, they should choose apps that they use regularly. If they aren't good at drawing, they can write the names of the apps in the rounded squares.
- Tell them they are going to prepare to give a short presentation about each one. This could be for as little as 20 seconds each, PechaKucha-style, which is realistic for low level students and will help higher-level students be focused in what they say. You needn't impose such a strict time-limit, however.
- As part of the preparation, and bandwidth permitting, allow students to visit the app stores on their devices to read about the functionality of the apps they have chosen. They can mine the authentic text for lexis, which will help to "scaffold" what they want to say at the next stage.
- Display the worksheets round the walls in an "art gallery". Students should circulate and guess who selected each set of 6, based on what they know of each other. At the end of this stage, the originators of each worksheet reveal their identities.
- Now, in small groups (3+ individuals) the students give the short talks about their 6 apps and their reasons for choosing them. The others in the group who are listening can be encouraged to suggest another app they know that the speaker may like or be interested in – this could also become an extension task: see below.

Task: Option 2

- This option focuses more narrowly on one or two of the apps, and can be run in small groups or as class presentations.
- The students will present the app(s) in more depth, walking those in the group through its key features of the how they have used them. This will be a kind of sales pitch, assuming that the members of the audience know little about the app concerned. (The more you can encourage students to choose an app which is specific to them, and unfamiliar to others, the better.)
- After the short presentation, the listeners ask questions to discover more about the app – its features and bugs – to see if they would like to use it themselves.
- At the end, everyone reports back about one previously unfamiliar app that they would be interested in trying out.

5d My life in apps

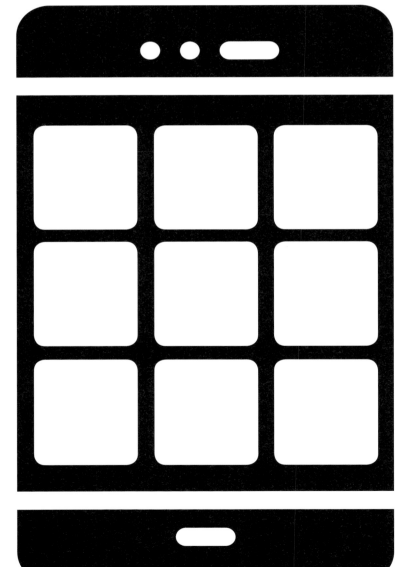

For each of the apps you have selected, make notes about:

- why you chose it;

- how often you use it;

- what you use it for;

- what its *best features* are;

- whether there is anything that could be added to improve it.

ACTIVITIES FOR TASK-BASED LEARNING
by Neil Anderson and Neil McCutcheon

© DELTA Publishing, 2019 | www.deltapublishing.co.uk
ISBN 978-3-12-501701-6

5e Heroes

 About the activity

Task type	long turn, reaching a decision
Task outcome	Students speak about someone that they admire then vote for the person who most deserves the award.

Introduction

The task encourages students to think about qualities they admire in people more generally, and then to nominate someone for the award and make a "pitch" for that person. In our experience, some students find it easy to think of public figures and celebrities to nominate; others prefer to talk about people in their own immediate family and circle of friends. For people who say they aren't the type to have heroes, steer them away from celebrities and in the direction of everyday talent, altruism and determination.

Variation, extension, task repetition

- The idea of "icons" or role-models may appeal to teenagers, depending on the age and attitudes of your group. In our experience, YLs class have been (perhaps surprisingly) resistant to this, and prefer to choose someone from their family or immediate circle of friends.
- Eulogies. Adults who know each other well may enjoy "lighting a candle" for a relative or friend who is no longer alive. (Of course, this should not be as a candidate for an award, but simply a matter of sharing their feelings and reflecting on this person's life.) Remove all elements of competition and look for the admirable qualities the people have in common. Note that in this variation, students will possibly unearth some material they have not shared much, and so could become emotional. While this kind of personal involvement with a task is a good thing, you will want to avoid the classic mistake of giving insensitive language feedback at a point when you should be listening to *what* the student is telling you.

Language feedback options

- Vocabulary for personal characteristics (See lead-in).
- Language to talk about achievements: is *famous/ well-known/much admired for…, stood out from the crowd, campaigned for justice, took a stand, exceptionally talented, had an enormous influence/impact on, never gave up, determined, had the courage of their convictions*
- Present perfect (contrasted with past) tenses: *has been really influential, has stood the test of time… X was the first person to… She began at a time when…*
- Time adverbials for periods and points in time: *between 1962 and 1970, in the nineties, for most of our lives, over the past few years, since 2016*
- Superlatives: *the __est (X) of all time*

▶ How to run the activity

Levels	B1–C2
Ages	any
Length	30 minutes

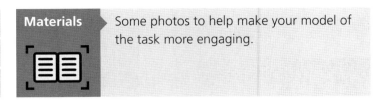

Materials — Some photos to help make your model of the task more engaging.

Pre-task

- Display photographs of people who have achieved something special in their respective fields, and ask students who the people are and what they are famous for. It's good at this stage to vary some obvious choices more obscure ones; if students don't recognise some of the people, they will naturally want to ask you questions about why you've decided to include them in the "gallery".
- This open class stage should lead to certain relevant language about personal characteristics (see language focus, below). This should be clarified and recorded since it will inevitably be useful for the main task.
- If you like, students can brainstorm other characteristics that they think are admirable. These are too complicated to rank, but some students like to discuss what might be the positive and negative aspects of a quality like generosity or tolerance, for example. (Do you know anyone who is *generous to a fault?*) Encourage them to think of concrete examples.

Main task

- Students have to choose someone they would like to put forward for the award. You can restrict the award to a particular field, such as politics, sport, or entertainment. You may wish to exclude people who are just too obvious in certain countries or cultural contexts; the task will work best if you have a range of nominations.
- You should provide a model by playing the accompanying recording. If you postpone this stage, however, until after the students have chosen their candidate, they will be less influenced by your choice!
- It's a good idea to add a stage where students research something about their chosen person. This is a link to some famous icons:
  https://www.bbc.co.uk/programmes/profiles/xfhZH9qWPt1G8F2mbN2fVc/meet-the-icons
- This is a good link for some lesser known choices:
  http://www.bbc.co.uk/programmes/articles/2HD4HmbL3Dxnkvv5nJSDmCj/witness-collections
- Now, in small groups, students make their pitches. The listeners can be encouraged to ask questions, and then the groups should vote for the nominee they prefer. These nominees go forward into the next (whole class) round. The person who successfully nominated person X now repeats their presentation for the whole class. Finally, the class votes for who wins. (For more discussion, they can talk in pairs about the reasons for their choice before the final vote.)

5f Happy accidents

 About the activity

Task type	information gap
Task outcome	Students tell each other about two (or more) key events in their lives which have had important results.

This task is about counterfactuals and serendipity. It encourages students to think about important crossroads and happy accidents in their lives, and the effects of these small chances on the rest of their lives. It is a **focused task** in that it inevitably generates examples of unreal conditionals of various kinds – though in a context that usually avoids conversations about regrets.

Variation, extension, task repetition

- **Lucky breaks** In a different version of the task, you will need the story of someone's career. Provide a short version of this, or encourage students to use online resources to read about the (early) career of someone whom they admire. They should look for any key decisions or "lucky breaks" that helped them get noticed. Some of the most interesting ones are those that are simply luck, but look with hindsight as though they were meant to be.

  > E.g. Steve Jobs made friends with Steve Wozniak when they were both working at Hewlett-Packard – Jobs was an intern there for a summer – and they started the Apple company together. He dropped out of college and began working on video games design. Perhaps if he had continued with his studies, they would never have started the company.

- **Counterfactuals in history** This version works with advanced students with some knowledge of history or current affairs. Ask them to think about which events in (recent) history were the most important ones for the development of the modern world.

Language feedback options

- Unreal conditionals (3rd and mixed): *If I hadn't tried to steal the cheese, we wouldn't have become friends / we might not have met.*
- The "future in the past" *We would become close friends; We went on to record a lot of music together*
- Sequencers: *At first we didn't get on, It wasn't until .... that I realised..., As a result, Afterwards, A few years later..., Eventually..., We ended up -ing.*
- Narrative tenses (for the short personal anecdotes)
- Present perfect (for the results that bring the story up to date)

▶ **How to run the activity**

Levels	B2 +
Ages	adults
Length	30 minutes

Materials	Worksheet 5f

Pre-task

- Most students will not be aware of the film **Sliding Doors** (1998), starring Gwyneth Paltrow, but this is good for creating the context. You might like to show them one of the trailers on YouTube to give them the general idea that the film hinges on; the split-second moment that affects whether Paltrow's character catches or misses a train has huge repercussions on her future – and both versions are shown.
- As an alternative to, or in addition to, showing the trailer, tell them about an incident in your life, perhaps trivial-seeming at the time it occurred, but one which has had important consequences. The easiest contexts to think about were the times when you met people who went on to become close friends (or your life partner).

> *When I was at University, we were having a party on our landing in our halls of residence one evening. Everybody had drunk a little bit, and had started to do some silly things. I remember being hungry and, looking out of the window, I saw on a windowsill, a lump of cheese. (We didn't have any easily accessible fridges in our block.) Someone had a hook – perhaps it was a coat hanger – and I lowered this down on a piece of string to try and reach the cheese. The person in the room below saw this happening, and their cheese about to disappear. So he ran upstairs to find out who was trying to steal it – a bit annoyed at first, but he ended up joining the party. This was James – and he and I became very close friends. In fact, we ended up writing and recording a lot of music together. If it hadn't been for the string and cheese incident, we might never have met.*

NB Unreal conditionals are likely to occur, though should not be focused on explicitly at this stage.

- Link to the next stage by telling students that the theme of the lesson is that "important changes are the result of small chances".

Main task

- Students now write down two (or more) important similar events in their lives. Allow enough note-taking/thinking time. You may need to monitor and prompt them with some suggestions.
- As the second part of the task, they need to think about the results of these happy accidents, which will include parts of their character and career that now seem immutable and "meant to be". The fun of the task comes from unearthing the chance origins of these.
- Run the task. Insist on a report stage, where the students can tell the class about their partner's story.

5f Happy accidents – my life

Where and when? How old were you? What happened on that day?	What are the results in your life *now?*
And the short-term result was…	

Where and when? How old were you? What happened on that day?	What are the results in your life *now?*
And the short-term result was…	

ACTIVITIES FOR TASK-BASED LEARNING
by Neil Anderson and Neil McCutcheon

5g Folk remedies

 About the activity

Task type	personalised information gap
Task outcome	Students share ideas for cold remedies (and other health tips) and decide which they think are most likely to be efficacious.

Introduction

Usually people carry around with them examples of homespun wisdom, handed down from parents and relatives, the effectiveness of which they are convinced of. In this task, students get a chance to compare and even question some of these ideas, beginning with prescriptions for fending off colds and infections. This task works well, even at lower levels, because it has a concrete focus and many students will have a clear idea of what they want to say.

Variations, extension, task repetition

- The main information-sharing part of the task can be done equally well in groups.
- The task can link to doctor-patient role-plays, which lower level students enjoy. To add spice to this, the "doctors" can be unconventional ones, and the patients can be encouraged to cast doubts on some of the advice they get.
- Higher levels can discuss the relative merits of pharmaceutical treatments and alternative medicine, including herbal remedies.

Language feedback options

- Infinitive of purpose and related expressions to express causal connections. *I wash my hands to avoid catching colds, lemon juice is (good) for* + noun phrase/ – ing, *this helps with X, sneezing into your elbow is so that other people don't…*
- The lexis of symptoms and treatment: *Catch/get colds/flu, avoid X/ prevent X (from – ing), a cure for, efficacious, works like a dream*
- Expressions for advice including modal auxiliary verbs: *should, have to, It's (not) a good idea to.*
- Various "real" conditionals and expressions with conditional meaning: *If you're on a flight with lots of ill people, there's a good chance of… Do that and you'll just get worse.*
- Some proverbs, which students always love: *An apple a day keeps the doctor away.*
- Adverbs and related phrases to do with certainty, and lack of it: *I swear by this. This is bound to make things worse; this invariably/inevitably helps. I'm a bit sceptical about this one, That's an old wives' tale.*

How to run the activity

Levels	A2 +
Ages	adults
Length	20 minutes

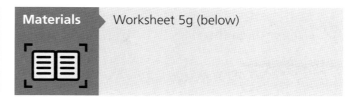

Materials	Worksheet 5g (below)

Pre-task

- You can begin by showing a picture of someone with a cold – and you may wish to include other symptoms here if you think they can be used as part of the task. Elicit related vocabulary – *have a cold, flu, stung by nettles, insect bite, hiccups…*
- If you have your own inherited "prescription" for any of these afflictions, choose one or two to share with students. (Alternatively, use the accompanying recording.) As they listen, they can think about whether they agree with you or not.

Main task

- The simplest version of the task is for students to think of their own examples. Encourage them to begin by thinking of what their mothers and grandmothers taught them. Are there any remedies that are specific to the place where they come from? We have usually focused on colds and viral infections, but if students are stuck for ideas, you can include any of the symptoms in the lead-in.
- Allow one or two minutes for students to plan what they would like to say, and be available to support them with any vocabulary they don't know. For students who don't have any ideas at all, encourage them to think more widely, for example, about very basic first aid – is it a good idea to rub antiseptic cream on a cut? Do they know any cures for hiccups?
- Now the students have to mingle and talk to as many others as they can in a given time frame. The idea is to collect (note down) ideas that they like the sound of, and that they think will work.
- In feedback to the task, everyone listens and decides which are the best ideas, and which they think are just *old wives' tales.*

Problem	Prescriptions	Do they work?

ACTIVITIES FOR TASK-BASED LEARNING
by Neil Anderson and Neil McCutcheon

5h Cook off!

 About the activity

Task type	long turn
Task outcome	Students swap recipes, and evaluate the recipes of others in a competition.

Introduction

In this task, students share and rate their favourite recipes. The format can be kept relatively simple or be "spiced up" to make it more competitive along the lines of popular cooking shows. Lower level students will enjoy the task, and we have found they can perform it quite successfully because of the communicative need (wanting to express their ideas) and the type of text, which is so familiar and straightforward. Students lower than B2 will, however, need substantial input: cooking vocabulary (verbs and utensils), and ingredients. This is provided as always at the pre-task stage, and as you monitor.

Variation, extension, task repetition

- Students produce written recipes, which can be displayed around the room for the competition stage.
- Students create a menu. This could be to suit different (defined) people or for a special occasion. For example, it's a visit by a local dignitary and her entourage. Some of them are vegetarians. (The more restrictions you put on the task, the more challenging it is.)

Language feedback options

- Cooking (verbs and utensils) – See the pre-task stage above.
- Quantifiers and modification of these: *quite a lot, a little (bit of), a large amount, just a spoonful of… will do, should be enough.*
- Words to describe tastes: *savoury, sweet, bitter, salty, sour, bland; the flavours balance complement each other.*
- Modification of adjectives: *It's far too sweet, it's not salty enough.*
- Imperatives and impersonal "you" for the instructions. *Sprinkle the X with salt, (you) turn down the heat, (you) leave it to simmer.*
- Sequencing adverbs: *First, next, at the very end…*
- Language to describe points and periods of time. *Turn the heat down and simmer for 20 minutes, Leave it until you see it bubbling, When it's cooked, you'll see the oil rise to the surface and then it's time to…*

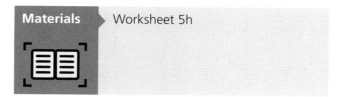

How to run the activity

Levels	A2 +
Ages	adults (possible also for teens)
Length	45 minutes +

Materials	Worksheet 5h

Pre-task

- Display some favourite dishes in an "art gallery" format round the walls. Your students can circulate and comment on which ones they think they would like/dislike; the origins nationality of the dishes and what they are called in English.
- In feedback, some relevant vocabulary will come up: e.g. *I really like fried food; It's better when you grill it.*
- You may need to teach vocabulary for food preparation *(slice, chop, dice, grate)* and different types of cooking *(fry, grill, boil, bake, simmer, stir, sprinkle)*. There is a lot here, but the concepts are mostly quite simple, so we have found the easiest way is through a picture-matching task. (If you don't have one to hand, search online for "ELT vocabulary food cooking" and look at the images tab.) You'll probably want to add some basic equipment and utensils *(pan, frying pan, oven, wooden spoon)*. Students can test each other on the words in pairs.

Task 1

- You should now provide an oral or written model of one of your favourite recipes. Note that the dish needn't be anything elaborate – beans on toast will do.
- The students' task is to listen and see if they think they would enjoy the dish you are describing. (Alternative tasks: Would they change any of the *ingredients*? Is it similar to a dish they make themselves?) If you like, you can have them make notes and recap the recipe with a partner as a rehearsal for the main task to follow.

Main task

- Students take some time to complete the worksheet with notes about a dish that they know how to prepare. Tell them that it needn't be something very complicated. You can put any spin on the task you like, as suitable for your group. Less experienced cooks can think of a dish that they know very well (a default meal). Others can describe one that they would make for guests, or one that is typical of their local area.
- Be prepared to circulate and help with other vocabulary at this stage; this will be necessary because of the wide variety of ingredients that might be involved.
- Next, students get together in groups and listen to each other's recipes. Listeners should give each idea a star-rating (out of 5) and suggest any variations i.e. an ingredient that they might add. The dish with the most points goes through to the next round.
- Repeat the last stage with a larger group or with the whole class.

5h Cook off!

A recipe for

Ingredients (and amount):

e.g. 225g of lentils
a tablespoonful of oil...

Method:

e.g. First, heat the oil...

Utensils:

e.g. A large pot and a frying
pan

ACTIVITIES FOR TASK-BASED LEARNING
by Neil Anderson and Neil McCutcheon

© DELTA Publishing, 2019 | www.deltapublishing.co.uk
ISBN 978-3-12-501701-6

6 Creative (design) tasks

6a Introducing the band

 About the activity

Task type	role-play
Task outcome	Students engage in an interview in role as band members and journalists.

Introduction

We grew up in an era when the idea of "celebrity" was reaching its zenith in the 1980s, but this task will work well with music fans of any age. It can also be done as a more general "celebrity" interview, or in fact any kind of interview. The main thing is to choose the context carefully to suit the interests of your class. Here, the learners assume fake identities as an imaginary band, and interviewers. They have to use their imaginations; in our experience, they can be very inventive and have a lot to say. The task can be also be used to supplement textbook units which focus on more conventional interview practice.

Variation, extension, task repetition

Other interview situations that work well:

- Students choose celebrities from film, sports, or other fields that they are interested in, and prepare individual interviews.
- Interviewing a babysitter, a house-sitter, a new flatmate for a shared house.

Younger learners may enjoy writing a band profile of their invented band, or of a band they are interested in, for a music website. This will recycle the language from the lesson.

Language feedback options

- A typical focus for this task would be the present perfect and progressive tenses, contrasted with the past simple and progressive. With lower level groups, you could narrow this focus.
- Focus the learners on sentences they used in your story that reveal different reasons for using the tenses. You could also use pre-prepared examples e.g.:

  - *We've been together for 4 years.*
  - *We've been touring a lot this year to promote our album.*
  - *Joshua and Rots met at school, and they started writing songs in music class.*

- Focus learners on the idea that the past simple is used for finished time and the present perfect for time "up till now". Show how *for and since* are used to refer to a period and point in time respectively.
- You could also provide some controlled practice to help learners discriminate between the new forms.
- Alternative or additional language focus: more time adverbials, question forms, indirect speech.

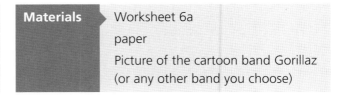

▶ How to run the activity

Levels	A2–B2
Ages	teens, young adult
Length	1 hour +

Materials	Worksheet 6a
	paper
	Picture of the cartoon band Gorillaz (or any other band you choose)

Pre-task

- Show the learners a picture of Gorillaz. Who could these characters be? (Perhaps someone will have heard of the band.) You could choose any band, of course, though we have found that because Gorillaz are not real, this prevents opinions from becoming polarised! Tell them something about the characters, or learners could simply comment on their looks and what instruments they might play.
- Elicit any essential key vocabulary that is unfamiliar, but will support the task: *release an album/single; go on tour; debut; appear on TV; get together; split up.*
- Optional stage: Tell learners that they are going to be a character in a band. They could draw their character, and choose a name – and instrument/s or role they want in the band. They now mingle to find the other band members. You could set a minimum or maximum number for this if you like.
- For shorter lessons, a tidier alternative is to sit the learners straight away in groups as the bands and (pairs of) interviewers.

Task

- Instruct task. Bands are to work out the details of their lives – not just their name and style of music, but when/how they met, and their career history, etc. Interviewers prepare the questions they want to ask. (Give out prompt sheets if you like – adapt from the examples below.)
- Run the MTV-style interviews. If all the students are in bands, following the third bullet above, then half of the class can be interviewers (with a prompt sheet) for the first round of interviews. This could take around 5 minutes, but sometimes lasts longer. The number of interviewers per band does not matter, but we have always found this works well with more than one.
- This stage is then repeated, with band members becoming the interviewers, and vice versa.
- Monitor, noting down examples of good language use and errors.
- An optional stage is a class "performance" of some of the interviews, which you can easily record using a mobile phone.

6a Introducing the band

You are in a famous band

After releasing several singles, you have finally got a number one hit. Now the whole world wants to know about you. You are going to be interviewed by a journalist from MTV. Decide:

- the name of your band _____
- The role of each band member (instruments played, how long you've known each other, how long you've played together)
- Your favourite CD releases (chart positions, release dates, failures and successes)
- The places you've toured (local or international, size of audiences, and funny stories from your concerts or tours.)
- The image you want to give MTV's audience (Are you crazy and dangerous, or laid back and cool?)

Remember to try and promote your new single – decide what it's called and when it's out, then mention it as many times as possible.

You are a journalist

You are going to interview a world famous band for MTV.
Before the interview, you need to plan the questions you will ask.
Think about:

- The role of each band member (instruments played, how long they've known each other, how long they've played together)
- Their CD releases (failures and successes)
- The places they've toured (local or international; size of audiences; what the band members do in their spare time while on tour)
- Any famous gossip about the band (boyfriends/girlfriends, affairs, rumours that they've decided to sack the lead singer, or split up)
- Future plans
- Anything else that will interest MTV's young and lively audience

Remember to ask questions to all of the band members.

Write your questions here:

© DELTA Publishing, 2019 | www.deltapublishing.co.uk
ISBN 978-3-12-501701-6

ACTIVITIES FOR TASK-BASED LEARNING
by Neil Anderson and Neil McCutcheon

6b Home exchange

 About the activity

Task type	Creative
Task outcome	Students "sell" their home by persuading other students of its desirability; to choose which home you wish to stay in.

Introduction

Couchsurfing, home exchanges – there are a plethora of options besides the more traditional when it comes to selecting holiday accommodation. This activity is a variant of the "Speed Dating" task type: learners present their imaginary homes to each other and try to find the partner who they are happiest to exchange with for a short break.

Variation, extension, task repetition

- Repetition is built into the task by design – assuming there is enough time, and enough motivation to continue, learners can repeat the presentation/listen cycle up to four or five times. If you follow the language focus suggestion above of providing input between cycles, this provides added challenge and incentive to polish each turn.
- Another option to stimulate learners who need an extra challenge between repetitions is to add new elements to the task each cycle. For example, encourage learners to challenge the presenter, <u>based on what they have already heard</u> e.g. *okay, but the last home was close to the beach. Why is yours better?*
- A good source of language would be a teacher model – this can be provided either before the first task or between tasks. Ask the learners to listen to you describing your home/location for gist (e.g. *would you like to stay here? Why, why not?*). Then ask them to listen again, noting useful phrases and adjectives.

Language feedback opportunities

- Basic language for describing the home: rooms, furniture, facilities, prepositions of place.
- Language for describing the local area e.g. *quiet neighbourhood, historic town, nearby beach, 5 minutes' drive from…*
- Evaluative language for "selling" such as positive adjectives (e.g. *modern, spacious, well-equipped* etc), collocations (e.g. *fully-furnished flat, overlooks/surrounded by green areas*).
- Functional language for recommendations e.g. *I think you'd really appreciate the…, there's a (X) nearby which you have to visit, everyone who visits loves the…, a major selling point is…, it's ideal for…*

 **How to run the activity**

Levels	A2–B2
Ages	teens + adults
Length	40–60 minutes

Materials	Worksheet 6b

Pre-task

- Either elicit the term *home exchange* or put it on the board and ask students to guess what they think it is.
- Ask your students to discuss this as an option for deciding on where to holiday and what accommodation to choose. In feedback, establish that sometimes home exchange adverts don't offer a full picture – there may be, for instance, problems with noise, traffic, heating, facilities etc.
- Tell your students everyone is going to describe a home to exchange, and that they will present this to other members of the class (one at a time); in the end, they will decide which home they would like to stay in for their holiday. You can choose how realistic or imaginary you want this to be.
- Give out the worksheet. Instruct the students to sketch out the layout of the home using the blank grid. Monitor and help with language here. Areas you may need to help with include lexis for rooms, furniture/features of a home (e.g. *terrace, Jacuzzi, mezzanine*), selling points (e.g. *spacious, breath-taking views of…*, *recently refurbished*) local amenities and attractions (e.g. *plenty of local cafes and restaurants, within walking distance of the beach* etc).
- Give the students two or three minutes to think about what the key information about the flat they wish to convey is, and in what order they will do so.

Task

- Line the students up in a ladder: As on one side, and Bs facing them. Tell them they will have around 3 minutes to a) show their home b) present its key features c) outline the local attractions. Remind them their goal is to make it seem very attractive. They want the other learners to choose it! Remind the listener they should find out more information to ensure they are getting the full picture.
- Tell As to start. After 4 minutes, signal that B should now take their turn.
- Once both A/B have presented and asked questions, move one side of the ladder down so each learner has a new partner. The cycle is then repeated – A presents, B listens and asks for more information; then B presents, and A listens.
- The ladder can run for as long as you feel students are motivated to present and listen. When you finish, ask the learners to sit down and report back to their partner some of the more/less attractive homes they heard about, as well as whether they think they did a good job of selling their own home.
- Finally, ask students to say which home they wish to stay in, and why. Determine if any students in the class have actually decided to exchange homes with each other.

6b Home exchange – your presentation plan

Draw the plan of your home below

Take notes to help with your presentation (remember, you want your home and area to sound attractive!)	
How many **rooms** are there? What **furniture and equipment** can we find in them?	
Name 3–5 things that make your home **special**.	
What is the **immediate neighbourhood** like, and why? E.g. quiet, peaceful, lively, green, full of cafés	
What is the broader **area** like? What can a visitor **do and see**? e.g. visit beaches, museums, parks, go cycling, climbing	
Give two or three **reasons** why someone should choose your home.	

ACTIVITIES FOR TASK-BASED LEARNING
by Neil Anderson and Neil McCutcheon
© DELTA Publishing, 2019 | www.deltapublishing.co.uk
ISBN 978-3-12-501701-6

6c Soundtracks

 About the activity

Task type	Creative
Task outcome	Students create, present and evaluate pitches for films.

Introduction

Music is a powerful stimulus for creativity and therefore provides an ideal starting point for a creative task. Soundtracks from films can be particularly powerful, as they are composed to do a variety of things: to conjure a particular mood or atmosphere, to arouse emotion on the part of the viewer, to reflect and complement the action unfolding on the screen…and more besides. In this task, the evocative power of film soundtracks is used to stimulate the design of a brief film pitch that students collaborate to create and later present.

Variation, extension, task repetition

- When students select which excerpt to focus on in step 3, you can take control by allocating one excerpt to half the class, and one to the other half. We find it generally works better, though, if students have some choice here (i.e. if they are able to select the track they are more motivated by).
- Note that it is perfectly fine to just use a single excerpt for the main task: we include two for greater variety of pitches later on, selecting two excerpts with a different feel, suggestive of different genres and scenes. One may be easier to manage, however, and we have found there is still sufficient variety in the pitches.
- Decide how important the voting at the end is, and how well it will work for your class. Really, the goal is for the students to present their ideas, and for others to listen and ask for further details – it is not essential to vote, it simply rounds off the experience pleasingly. You can decide whether students are allowed to vote for their own film or if this is prohibited.
- The task can form the starting point for longer project work in designing the film, or aspects of it: a poster, tag line, dialogue from sample scenes.

Language feedback options

- Expressions for describing films: *it is set in… it takes place in… the main character is…*
- Present simple for describing scenes/plot: *the robber gets out of the car… a man walks across a field…*
- Language for expressing impressions: *it sounds/feels like… it made me think of…I felt as if…* (pre-task and task step 2).
- Adjectives and other descriptive language for describing films and scenes: *exciting, tense, powerful, action-packed.*
- Adverbs and adverbial expressions for outlining a scene/plot: *At first… suddenly…later… in the end…*

▶ How to run the activity

Levels	B1–C2
Ages	all
Length	30–45 minutes

Materials	Worksheet 6c
	Three instrumental pieces of music: They should evoke different types of film.

Pre-task

- Ask the students if they can remember any famous soundtracks from films. Ask: *how important for you is a film soundtrack? Why is it important, or not so important?*
- Play an excerpt from a soundtrack. For the pre-task, it is a good idea to select something that is quite clearly suggestive of a particular mood/genre; and that shifts in dynamic, suggestive of action/activity.
- Ask the students to listen to the music with the following tasks: *What type of film is this? What is happening in this scene?* Play it and then allow the students to discuss their opinions in pairs before offering feedback. Here, ensure you get students to justify *why* the excerpt evoked a particular mood/genre.

Main task

- Tell students they are going to listen to two more excerpts from soundtracks, one after the other. Their task the first time they listen is to take notes in the first row of the worksheet: emphasise they should write whatever comes to mind in terms of mood or what they can "see". These will be used to help them discuss and create a movie to pitch to other groups.
- After they have listened, ask the students in pairs to share their ideas, adding to their own lists from their partner's. As they are doing so, play the two excerpts in the background to stimulate more ideas. Monitor and help with any vocabulary or ideas the students need.
- Regroup the students so they are in small groups – each group should select one of the two excerpts (perhaps the one they found most evocative).
- Each group should now collaborate: using their notes, they should work together to create their summary of the film, using the prompts in the remaining rows of the worksheet. Everyone should agree on the answers, and each student should take notes, as every member will be presenting their film to other students in the next phase. As they do this, play the excerpts on a loop in the background.
- Elicit the names of the films created onto the board. Regroup the students so they are in small groups but with *different* students who have created a different film. So, for instance, if the grouping from step 4 was AAA/BBB/CCC, it should now be ABC/ABC/ABC. Give each student 1 or 2 minutes to present their film; the listeners are free to ask further questions as they listen. Let them know the goal: they will select their favourite pitch at the end.
- Feedback – now it is time to vote for the different pitches! Go through the titles of the movies on the board, and ask for a show of hands for each one, noting the votes next to the title on the board. Each time, ask someone who voted for the pitch to explain briefly why they chose it.

6c Soundtracks – your summary

	Soundtrack 1	Soundtrack 2
Write any words / images / feelings that come to you as you listen		
What type of movie is it?		
Where is the movie or scene set?		
Who are the characters?		
What are some main actions / events?		
What's the title?		

© DELTA Publishing, 2019 | www.deltapublishing.co.uk
ISBN 978-3-12-501701-6

ACTIVITIES FOR TASK-BASED LEARNING
by Neil Anderson and Neil McCutcheon

6d Rate your stay

 About the activity

Task type	Creative
Task outcome	Students collaborate to create a review for a hotel.

Introduction

Have you ever read online reviews for restaurants or hotels? They can be useful and informative but it's safe to say there is room for improvement when it comes to the clarity and accuracy of the prose (whether or not English is the L1 of the reviewer!). This task is designed to help students practice this real-life skill.

Variation, extension, task repetition

- If you feel it is easier, students can look at a model text *before* they write the task. However, be careful that the desire to use specific language does not become the focus of the task.
- The topic can be changed from hotels to other types of accommodation (e.g. apartments, camp sites), or restaurants, cafés, museums, exhibitions etc.
- You could direct students to online reviews. Be careful if you do so – many of these are written in dubious/non-standard English. It may be better done in class, as a correction exercise – have students look at some pre-selected reviews and ask them to identify errors and elements they could improve.
- Task repetition can take the form of students *redrafting* their reviews, incorporating some of the language from the samples, or from teacher feedback.

> **Recommendations**
> - Word of mouth (friends, colleagues)
> - Professional online reviews
> - Amateur user reviews
> - Automated recommendations
> - Don't bother – just pick one randomly!

Language feedback options

See the sample reviews after the worksheet – these can be "mined" for the following language areas, or any others that appear valuable to your students:

- Lexis for describing hotel facilities/characteristics: *receptionist, staff, gym, pool, sauna, tea/coffee-making facilities, rooms* etc.
- Language for positive evaluations: *patient/polite/helpful staff, great service, great value, ideally located, superb value for money, clean/warm rooms, breakfast included*
- Language for negative evaluations: *sparsely furnished/damp/dirty rooms, X facility was out of order/unusable/was not working, X was not as advertised, a little basic/noisy.*
- Language for making recommendations e.g. conditionals: *if you are looking for great value etc then look no further; it's worth it if you are on a budget,* imperatives: *avoid!*
- Sequencing: *First (of all)… Finally,…, Pros:… Cons:…, All in all…Overall…*

▶ How to run the activity

Levels	B1+
Ages	adult
Length	45–60 minutes

Materials	Worksheets 6d
	You might want to bring extra photos of hotels and hotel facilities.

Pre-task

- Establish the topic of travelling. Ask students how they decide on what hotels to stay in, which restaurants to eat in, or which sights to visit. Elicit the list of recommendations in the box onto the whiteboard, and then ask the students in pairs to decide which are more/less useful and reliable.

Task 1

- Tell students they will be in pairs writing short reviews of an imaginary hotel – **The Grand Majesty Inn**. It will be up to them how positive or negative the review is. Other pairs will read and give a score for the review out of five, guessing based on the content how they felt about the experience.
- Brainstorm the kind of things reviewers write about when reviewing a hotel e.g. *noise, cleanliness/hygiene, professionalism of staff, facilities (e.g. restaurant, gym, pool), location, general upkeep/condition of the building.*
- Put students into pairs. Focus them on **A** on the worksheet: they should brainstorm five positive features of their stay, and five negative features. There should be some logic here e.g. not *polite staff* as well as *impolite staff*. Tell the pairs they will pick from these ideas when writing their review. Circulate to check pairs have some decent ideas. You might like to get them to look at online reviews for inspiration.
- Draw attention to the template **B**, asking them to identify the different features of an online review.

Main task

- Tell students they should agree on a rating out of five for their hotel, and then select the ideas they wish to include in their body.
- Ask them to collaborate to write their review, using **B** on the worksheet. Remind them we will be reading each other's writing, so they should write clearly and accurately. *Tell them not to indicate the rating yet – remind them this will be the task of the readers i.e. to predict the rating given.*
- As the students write their reviews, monitor and feed in any language they need to express their ideas. Allow around 10 minutes for this.
- When the time is up, ask them to fold the paper on the line above **B**. Gather them in and distribute them: either on the walls in the form of a gallery walk, or if you are short of time, give each one to a new pair. They should read, allocate a score and explain why they have done so.

6d Rate your stay – your review

THE GRAND MAJESTY INN

A:

Positive features	Negative features
e.g • friendly staff	**e.g.** • room was not that clean

B:

Subject:

Rating: ☆ ☆ ☆ ☆ ☆

ACTIVITIES FOR TASK-BASED LEARNING
by Neil Anderson and Neil McCutcheon

© DELTA Publishing, 2019 | www.deltapublishing.co.uk
ISBN 978-3-12-501701-6

6d Rate your stay – sample reviews for language feedback options

---

Subject: Avoid like the plague!

I admit I was attracted by the cheap price but it seems you get what you pay for. The staff were rude and unhelpful (the receptionist's favourite phrase was "it's not my responsibility"). Rooms were damp and there was mould on the walls; there were no coffee or tea making facilities as advertised, just an old, expensive coffee machine in the reception…and it was out of order during our stay. Worst of all, NONE of the promised facilities were usable – the pool was empty, the sauna could not be used, and the "gym" had one exercise bike that was broken. Avoid!

Rating: ☆ ☆ ☆ ☆ ☆

Subject: Cheap and cheerful

First of all, the location is great – very close to the centre of town, with plenty of restaurants and bars nearby. This means, though, that it can be a little noisy – our room looked out onto the street. The rooms are a little basic but clean, and towels and bedding were changed every day. Facilities are limited but I don't think you can expect more for the price we paid. Finally, I should say the staff were very helpful in general – we had problems with ordering taxis to the airport and they solved this for us. All in all, it's worth it if you are on a budget.

Rating: ☆ ☆ ☆ ☆ ☆

Subject: HIGHLY RECOMMENDED!!

If you are looking for great value, great service, clean rooms and a perfect location then LOOK NO FURTHER! The Grand Majesty Inn offers superb value for money and is ideally located just behind the main square. Pros: the rooms were clean and warm, breakfast was included in the price with a huge range of hot and cold buffet options, and the staff were patient, polite and helpful. Cons: the rooms are perhaps a bit sparsely furnished, and the coffee machine was not working. Overall, though, fantastic value for the price.

Rating: ☆ ☆ ☆ ☆ ☆

6e The struggling artist

 About the activity

Task type	Creative
Task outcome	a) Students interpret and agree upon the message behind a painting. b) Students try to persuade others to buy their "masterpiece".

Introduction

This task can seem somewhat mean – you ask your students to draw something ("anything!") without telling them they will have to go on to sell this "masterpiece". We've found this adds to the fun: there's plenty of amusement to be had in persuading others to buy a picture that may not actually be very pleasing to look at. The real creativity, though, does not lie in drawing the picture but in deciding what each picture means, and in students persuading others to buy their particular work of art.

Variation, extension, task repetition

- Task 2 is a desirable but non-essential element if you are short of time: it can be omitted, or you can pick up on it the next lesson. In fact, picking up on it in the next lesson may be desirable if you plan to do a substantial language focus after Task 1 – this will relate to the first two language focus points above; the rest are relevant to Task 2.
- In another variation, move straight to Task 2, but tell students they are *art dealers* and they have to sell the (anonymous) picture they are given – usually the signatures are illegible. There is a prize for the dealer who gets the biggest pledge. It's also fun to reveal the identity of the artist behind the picture.
- If you wish to repeat Task 1, you can bring in ambiguous pictures, or ask for students to search for them on their phones. Searching for something like *strange pictures* will yield plenty of sites/articles that can be used (but check this in advance in terms of suitability for your students!).

Language feedback options

- Lexis related to the details of each picture.
- Lexis for art: *representational, abstract, an early work, a masterpiece, my blue period, symbolic, naïve, an original, up-and-coming, established artist.*
- Modals and other language for speculating/giving opinions about the details and message: *it looks as if it's (some sort of animal), it may/might/could be (a castle), it seems to be about (life), I have no idea what the message is/what it is saying, I'm not sure but I think it's about* etc.
- Language for persuading others: *it's well worth (it/the price) because…, you won't find a better picture/representation of (a cat), deep/profound/moving/a work of genius* etc.
- Responding to salesmanship: a) positive overtures: *that makes sense, I think you've convinced me, you're very persuasive* b) tactful rejection or hedging: *maybe I'll buy it; I'll think about it; let me decide later* c) direct rejection: *no, thanks, it's not my kind of picture/it's not to my taste/it's (just) not worth (it/the price)*

▶ How to run the activity

Levels	A1+
Ages	Teenagers and adults
Length	30–60 minutes*

Materials	Blank A4 paper: You should provide enough for each student. A means of sticking the paper around the room: This could, for example be, drawing pins, Blu Tack, Sellotape/Scotch Tape, or magnets.

* Task 2 can be done in a separate lesson or omitted.

Pre-task

- This task is better off "deep end" – it benefits from not having a lengthy lead-in on the topic (art/struggling artists).
- Put a blank A4 piece of paper under the chair of each student before the class starts. Then, when you start the activity, say you would like them to draw something. Be deliberately vague e.g. *draw anything you like. Whatever is in your head!* Give them 3 or 4 minutes for this. It can help to play some gentle music in the background as they draw and draw something on the board yourself.

Task 1

- Tell students they are actually artists: struggling/poor artists. They have just drawn their masterpiece. They should now write down three things on the paper: a) its title b) its value c) their signature.
- Tell them this is not in fact a classroom, but an art gallery. Ask the students to put their work on the wall somewhere (if this is not possible, they can put them on their chairs). Once the room is arranged, set the task: they should find a partner, and walk around the room, admiring the masterpieces. Put these questions on the board: *what can they see in the picture? What is the real "message" behind the picture?* Use your example on the board to demonstrate, eliciting these things. Give students 5–10 minutes to do this.

Task 2

- Tell students they should now try to persuade someone else to buy their masterpiece. Give them one or two minutes thinking time – they should decide why it is worth the value they gave it, and think of how to sell this to others.
- Line the students up in a ladder, so pairs are facing each other – line **A** and line **B**. **A** will go first – they should hold up the picture and then they have about 1 or 2 minutes to present it, trying to persuade **B** to buy it. **B** can ask follow-up questions. Demonstrate this using your picture on the whiteboard. Then they will switch roles, with **B** telling **A** about their picture.
- Time them – after each round, give a signal for the partner to start. When a pair has presented to each other, move one line of the ladder down so everyone has a new partner. The process is repeated – at least 3 times if possible, though this will depend on time and the number of students. Note they don't need to decide which picture they wish to buy until feedback.
- In feedback, simply ask the students which one they decided to buy and why. Assuming the atmosphere is positive and there is a good rapport among students, you can find out why they chose *not* to buy some of them e.g. too expensive.

6f Elevator pitch

 About the activity

Task type	Mingle and role-play
Task outcome	Students think of a proposal for a business venture and compete for "patrons".

Introduction

An elevator pitch is a proposal for a creative or business-related project that you can make to a potential backer in the time that an elevator ride takes. Finding backers for personal projects has never been easier than in the era of crowdfunding, with a number of websites dedicated to this. Everything depends on the originality of the idea and how persuasive you can be.

Variation, extension, task repetition

- Time-limits are flexible. You can decide to reduce the time as the activity progresses to make it more like an elevator pitch.
- The activity could be done as a short piece of writing, similar to those found on the websites. The pieces of writing are displayed (or shared electronically) before student make their choice.
- You can make the final stage into more of a role-play, along the line of reality television shows, with four judges who pronounce on the different ideas.

Language feedback options

- Topic-specific language: See pre-task.
- Adjectives and other lexis to describe the projects: *innovative, ground-breaking, X will appeal to…* *The best thing about X is… It comes with a handy… X contains/includes…*
- Passives: *It's inspired by, made in/of, designed for people who need to…*
- Language to describe purpose: *It's a new way to… One unique feature is… What makes this special is…*
- Functional language to do with making the pitch and responding: *I'm asking people to donate… Would you be interested in…? I'm not all that interested in… It's a good idea but Xs aren't really my thing*
- Questions, including indirect questions, to ask for further information: *Could you tell me if…*

 **How to run the activity**

Levels	B1–C2
Ages	teens, young adult
Length	30 minutes

Materials	Worksheet 6f
	Post-its

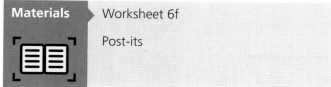

Pre-task

- To introduce the topic, you could show a still from a programme in which entrepreneurs pitch their business ideas to expert judges. At the same time, you could show the names of *crowdfunding* websites. Ask the students what the images have in common. Do they know anything that has been funded in this way? Perhaps they have themselves been a patron.
- You can pre-teach related vocabulary e.g. *entrepreneur, patron, backer, invest(or), pitch, fund, start-up, creative project.*
- Let students search the websites if this is possible. It's important to give them exposure to the range of ideas out there: gadgets and accessories; computer games; photo-books; a musical that someone wants to stage. The short texts are also good sources of linguistic input. NB Sometimes the ideas are described in a complicated way so it's a good initial task to discover just *what* is being proposed.

Task 1

- Students search for an example that they find attractive or useful. Would they fund it? They can summarise and then describe the idea to others in the class.

Main task

- Introduce the task. The students have to pitch their own idea to others in the class. First, they make some notes on the worksheet attached, and it's good if they write the title of the idea on a post-it for later. At this stage, they are likely to need some help with vocabulary and with the ideas themselves. (Whether or not you have done Task 1, they can get inspiration from another idea on one of the sites; a lot of the best ideas are derivative anyway.)
- Tell the students that investors will have € 250 to invest; they can split the sum between various projects or give it all to one.
- Students mingle, ideally moving on at your time signal, pitch their ideas and noting the ones they like best on the back of the worksheet.
- Once they have talked to a good number of others in the class, stick the post-it notes to a window or the whiteboard. Tell students they have € 250 to invest and they have to decide which ideas to back, and how much money to give to each. They can pledge these sums on other (different coloured) post-its and attach them to the ideas they are backing.
- In a final report stage, students explain their choices and the winner is the person who has attracted the largest sum, or largest number of pledges. (For teenage classes, specify clearly in advance how the winner will be decided.)

6f Elevator pitch – your plan

What's your creative or business project?

This is your chance to get patrons (backers). Make notes under the following headings to help you with your pitch.

My idea and why it's special. (Mention any unique selling points.)

Target market/audience

How much money you need to pledge. Can patrons contribute at different levels? What's in it for your patron? e.g. a free gift, lifetime membership, their name on the credits

ACTIVITIES FOR TASK-BASED LEARNING
by Neil Anderson and Neil McCutcheon
© DELTA Publishing, 2019 | www.deltapublishing.co.uk
ISBN 978-3-12-501701-6

7 Whole class

Dictogloss and retranslation: four sample texts for Chapter 7

These texts can be used for several activities in this section.

The angry golfer (sample B1–B2 level text)

John was having a very bad game of golf; on every hole, he'd hit the ball into the rough, or a bunker. Finally, after he'd hit an easy shot into the lake, he became so angry that he picked up his golf bag and threw it into the water. He was walking back to the car when he remembered he'd put the car keys in the same bag.

Three wishes (sample A2–B1 level text)

What would I wish for if I had three wishes? First of all, I'd wish for world peace, and an end to all wars and fighting. Second, I'd ask for a big house in the country for every member of my family, so they could live comfortably. For my third wish, I'd ask for ten more wishes.

What to do if you encounter a bear (sample B2–C1 level text)

The first, crucial piece of advice is this: neither run up to the bear and draw attention to yourself, nor try to hide or pretend you're not there. A surprised bear is a dangerous bear, so if it knows you are there, yet you do not seem to be a threat, the chances are it will mind its own business. Once you know it has spotted you, assuming it doesn't run away, then you should back away, facing the bear, and ensuring you make no sudden movements. It's highly likely the bear will lose interest in you as you fade into the distance.

A morning person (sample A1–A2 level text)

I usually wake up at 6.00 in the morning. I get up at about 6.30 and then I do some exercise on my exercise bike. I shower, I get dressed and then I make a cup of coffee, with milk and no sugar. I drink the coffee and watch the news. Then it's time to take the bus to work.

7a Dictogloss

 About the activity

Task type	Text reconstruction and comparison
Task outcome	Students collaborate to reconstruct a short text.

Introduction

Dictogloss is the most well-known of the text reconstruction procedures outlined here. Even so, it is not well represented in most major coursebooks. Given this and the fact that it is task-based (the goal being the reconstruction and analysis of a text), it would be remiss of us to omit it here. In this procedure, students listen to and then reconstruct a short text, collaborating to capture the sense of the original text. Their version is then compared to the original, and any differences in content, language and style are analysed.

Variation, extension, text repetition

- A key variation is doing the Dictogloss as a **flash reading.** This involves changing steps 1 and 2 in the main task above: instead of reading the text out loud, you should either project the text so all students can see it (or allow them to look at a paper copy) – but only for 30 seconds or so, before removing the text from view. The students then note as many key words and phrases as they can before collaboratively reconstructing the text.
- Dictogloss is also known as grammar dictation – this is indicative of one its central purposes i.e. to encourage students to **grammaticise** the key words into a cohesive and coherent text, and in doing so, notice the gap between the forms they have used and those in the original text. The process of creating a cohesive text is a task – use of specific linguistic forms is not key here. However, the language focus phase can involve attention to pre-selected grammatical forms: ones which are evident in the original text.
- Rules of thumb for creating a dictogloss text (see the four samples):
  - Keep it short – between 50 and 100 words.
  - Ensure it is not too lexically complex.
  - Make sure the text is coherent and cohesive.

Language feedback options

- Narrative tenses (past simple/past progressive/past perfect/*would*);
- Lexical patterns *he was so* .... *(that) he* .... *;*
- Cohesive devices (articles, reference, substitution e.g. *the same*).

▶ How to run the activity

Levels	A2–C1
Ages	teenagers and adults
Length	30 minutes

Materials	Worksheet 7a (optional)
	A short text (approximately 50–100 words) on a handout or projected
	Paper or computer
	Guiding questions for the desired post-task language focus

Pre-task

(The pre-task procedure is based on *The angry golfer* sample dictogloss text but can be adapted to reflect the content of the particular text used.)

- Ask students what sports they play in their free time, before asking if anyone has ever played golf. Tell them they are going to listen to a short text about an angry golfer. Ask them to discuss in pairs what can go wrong while playing golf.
- Pre-teach, as necessary, based on feedback to the pair discussion: *hole, rough, bunker, golf bag.*

Main task

- Read the short text to the students, at normal speed. Ask them to listen and check if any of their ideas from the pre-task were correct.
- Read the short text again – this time, instruct the students to pick up a pen as soon as you have finished reading the text; they should then note as many key words and phrases as they can remember. *Note:* whenever you read the text, be careful not to read the text too slowly, or too often: the idea is for learners to deploy their own linguistic resources to reconstruct the text, so it is important they are when listening mostly catching key content words.
- Ask the students to work in pairs or threes – they should pool their notes/key words and attempt to reconstruct the text. Appoint one of the learners in each group as the secretary while making it clear that all students should contribute and agree on the version they are reconstructing. Give the goal: they should aim to create a similar text, as close as possible to the original in terms of the information included. As students do this, monitor to see if they have a sufficient number of key words/phrases to make a good attempt at recreating the text.
- If it seems necessary to do so, read the text one more time (be careful though not to turn the procedure into a traditional dictation – if they are by now recreating the original reasonably well there is no need to read it again).
- Option: allow students in a group to join with another group to compare current reconstructions, adding and refining them further.
- After they have completed their reconstruction, hand out/project the original text and ask them to compare their version with the original: *did you include all the information? Did you miss any information? Was the order of information the same?*

7a Sample template for Dictogloss: The angry golfer

A: Our final text

------- (fold here) -------

B: Original text

- *Underline the verbs in your text and this text.*
- *Did you use the same tense?*
- *What is the difference in meaning between your tense and the tense used below?*

John was having a very bad game of golf; on every hole, he'd hit the ball into the rough, or a bunker. Finally, after he'd hit an easy shot into the lake, he became so angry that he picked up his golf bag and threw it into the water. He was walking back to the car when he remembered he'd put the car keys in the same bag.

ACTIVITIES FOR TASK-BASED LEARNING
by Neil Anderson and Neil McCutcheon
© DELTA Publishing, 2019 | www.deltapublishing.co.uk
ISBN 978-3-12-501701-6

7b Decon-Recon

 About the activity

Task type	Text reconstruction
Task outcome	Students reconstruct a text in continuous prose based on fact sentences.

Introduction

Deconstruct-Reconstruct, more commonly known as "Decon-Recon" is a less commonly known type of text reconstruction task – in this case, learners collaborate to break down a short cohesive text into a series of simple sentences, each one containing a single piece of information from the original; after an appropriate time delay, learners in groups collaborate to reconstruct the text, before comparing their reconstructed version with the original version. The time delay between deconstruction and reconstruction is vital, as the learners should not recreate the fully cohesive text immediately from memory. It's important, rather, that they actively employ the language they have at their disposal to reconstruct the text, as this is how they will come to notice gaps in their active linguistic repertoire. I would suggest a minimum of an hour between deconstructing and reconstructing

Variation, extension, task repetition

- To repeat the task, the students could be asked to put away the text, and then try to reconstruct the text again, using just key words you put on the board e.g. *car / air / crash / second floor / office building etc*.
- They could alternately devise their own story, using the linguistic structures focused on in the language focus phase.
- As with dictogloss, a short text – 50 words or so – works effectively, and challenge can be increased by reducing the number of sentences in the text (one long complex sentence makes the task harder – see the examples below).
- It often works well if you do the deconstructing in the final 20 minutes of one lesson, as a cooler, and then move to the reconstructing and post-task phases in the next lesson.

Language feedback options

Ask the learners to look at the language area you feel is useful for them, and that you have included in your text. As appropriate to the level / text ask questions such as:
- *Are the sentences longer in your text or the original? Why are they longer in the original?*
- *Find words similar to "and" or "but" or "so" or "because".*
- *Underline words such as "who", "which" – where could you use them in your text?*
- *Did you use "before" and "after"? What comes next – a verb, a noun or both?*

▶ How to run the activity

Levels	A1+	**Materials**	Worksheet 7d (optional)
Ages	any		Paper
			Computer
Length	30 minutes		Guiding questions for the desired post-task language focus

Pre-task

- Draw/show a picture related to the story: in the case of the sample text for this procedure, a car stuck in the second floor wall of an office building.
- Pre-teach any key phrases that may block understanding and which will facilitate the prediction in step 3. For the higher levels sample text below, I suggest e.g. *central barrier, become airborne.*
- Ask the learners in pairs to guess in pairs how the situation in the picture happened. Put some ideas onto the whiteboard.
- Project or give the short text to students and set a strict time limit – they should skim for about 10 seconds to see if any of their ideas were correct.
- Elicit some personal response to further build interest – *why do you think the man fell asleep? What do you think the police should do?*

Task

- Ask the learners how many sentences there were in the original text (one). Tell them that in pairs they are going to deconstruct the text into short sentences. Each sentence should usually have one piece of information in it; no more than two. They should finish with between 10 and 15 short sentences.
- Then, in pairs or small groups, ask the learners to write their fact sentences on a piece of paper separate from the text; let them know they should write their names on top and that you are going to collect the papers.
- Monitor and check the students are doing this e.g. each sentence is just a single piece of information.
- When they have finished, take the papers in. Tell the students you will come back to the second half of the task (reconstructing the text) later on in this lesson, or in a later lesson (as suits your timetable).
- After the delay, ask them in pairs to orally recall what the text was about. Then hand out the papers to the correct groups, having instructed them that to finish the task, they must now *reconstruct* the text from the simple sentences back into a cohesive text.
- Students then reconstruct the text as best they can, using their sentences. Monitor to check they are using all the information and doing so in the right number of sentences (if they are struggling, relax the rules – it is okay, if they are stuck, to use one or two more sentences than the original text).
- After they have completed this, hand out/project the original text and ask them to compare their version with the original. Encourage them to underline any differences that seem significant.

7b Decon-Recon – sample texts

Higher levels (B2–C1)
(This text is a single sentence.)

A car flew into the air before crashing into the second floor of an office building last night in California, as a result of the driver, who fell asleep at the wheel after having been on the road for many hours, hitting the central barrier, which caused the car to become airborne, before hitting the office, which was at the time closed, meaning nobody was injured including, luckily, the driver.

Intermediate levels (B1–B2)
(This text has two sentences.)

A car flew into the air before crashing into the second floor of an office building last night, after the driver, who fell asleep at the wheel, hit the central barrier. As a result, the car became airborne, before hitting the office, which was at the time closed, so nobody was injured because of the crash.

Lower levels (A2–B1)
(This text has four sentences.)

A car crashed into an office building last night. The driver, who was asleep, hit the central barrier, and the car flew into the air. It then crashed into the office, which was closed. Because no one was working, no one was injured.

© DELTA Publishing, 2019 | www.deltapublishing.co.uk
ISBN 978-3-12-501701-6

ACTIVITIES FOR TASK-BASED LEARNING
by Neil Anderson and Neil McCutcheon

7c Retranslation

 About the activity

Task type	Text reconstruction
Task outcome	Students compare two texts and examine them for similarities in content, cohesion and form.

Introduction

Retranslation shares clear similarities with the other types of text reconstruction tasks we have seen so far: as with **Dictogloss**, a short text is involved; as with **Decon-Recon,** there needs to be a time delay between the two main phases of the activity. Here, though, strictly, it's not reconstruction that is involved but **retranslation:** students first translate a short text from English into L1; and then, after a time delay, from L1 back into English. The pedagogical principles and benefits are the same: it is collaborative, involves multiple skills, attention to meaning, form and cohesion, and potentially allows students to notice the gap between the language they used and the language forms in the original text. We first came across Retranslation in a 1984 ELTJ article by Julian Edge.

Variation, extension, task repetition

- *What if I don't share my students' L1?* We have not found this to be a significant problem: the key, as with any task, is to set it up so that students collaborate more or less independently of the teacher. You should also, if you do know the students' L1, resist the urge to intervene and teach too much during the translation and retranslation phases: this creates the risk of no gaps to notice! However, there is no doubt that if you do know the L1, you can offer some useful guiding interventions along the lines of… *that's not quite how we say it in German though – we use a different verb. Can you think which one?*
- *What if my class is multilingual?* This creates a bigger practical problem, but so long as there are two students with the same L1, the task remains collaborative and they can be grouped accordingly: the text comparison stage actually benefits from students then being mixed up so that the groups are heterogeneous – they can then identify what they have translated differently, and why. If the class includes one or more individuals who alone speak a particular language, step 2 in the main task is best set for homework, with the retranslation and text comparison phases occurring in the next lesson.

Language feedback options

- Collocations/expressions: *crucial (piece of) advice, draw attention to yourself, mind (its) own business, back away, sudden movement, lose interest in, fade into the distance*
- Lexical parallelism: *a surprised bear is a dangerous bear*
- Participle clauses: *facing the bear…, ensuring you…*
- Adverbs and conjunctions: *neither… nor; yet…; assuming (that)…*
- Expressing probability: *the chances are… it's highly likely that…*

▶ How to run the activity

Levels	B1 +*
Ages	teen – adult (monolingual group)
Length	30–45 minutes**

Materials	Short text to be translated into L1: This should be on a handout or projected.
	Paper
	Computer

* though shorter simpler texts can be used for lower levels. (See Dictogloss sample texts.)
The example here is for B2 or C1.

** with a time delay necessary halfway through (e.g. translate in one lesson, retranslate in the next)

Pre-task

(The pre-task example is based on **What to do if you encounter a bear** sample dictogloss /retranslation text but can be adapted to reflect the content of the particular text used)

- Ask students to imagine a situation: they are walking in the forest when suddenly, 5 or 6 metres away, they see a bear. It doesn't yet seem aware of them. What should they do? Students discuss in pairs the best way to react. Feedback – elicit their ideas onto the board, creating a mind map.
- Tell students to listen to you reading a short text (see **What to do if you encounter a bear**). As they listen, they should look at the mind map to see any of the ideas on the board are mentioned in the text. Check this in feedback.
- Elicit some personal reactions to the text: *do you agree with the suggestions in the text? Are they better than yours or not?*

Main task

- Put the students in pairs or groups of three. Give out the text you have just read to them and set the task: they should collaborate to translate it into their mother tongue. Set guidelines: they should aim to use expressions and forms that feel natural in L1, so long as what they write captures the original information in more or less the correct order. They are free to use dictionaries on their phones to check words and phrases.
- As the students work on the task, monitor to help with any vocabulary needed, and troubleshoot any other issues that occur. If students are discussing the best way to translate something, facilitate this.
- After 15–20 minutes, ask the students to write their names/group name on the piece of paper containing the translation, and then collect in the texts, telling the students you will return to this later.
- *Either* later in the lesson *or* the next lesson, hand out the texts (it is important that there is at least an hour gap between initial translation and retranslation; longer if possible).
- Students then retranslate the text back into English. Monitor to check they are using all the information and again, troubleshoot any problems/disagreements, though let the students make the ultimate decision about phrasing, word placement etc. They then compare it with the original text and talk about any differences.

7d Text reconstruction

 About the activity

Task type	Text reconstruction
Task outcome	Students collaborate to reconstruct a text using key phrases in the same order given.

Introduction

This is similar to **Decon Recon** – in fact, it is in essence **Decon Recon** without the Decon: students examine a series of key words and phrases and are tasked with turning these into a coherent text, using the words in the order they are provided. Like the others in this section, students are called on to **grammaticise** – that is, to add the necessary grammar to the key words. This creates potential for them to **notice** gaps in their knowledge when they later compare their text with the original.

Variation, extension, activities

- Asking the students to use the key words/phrases in the order they appear places restrictions on the task; if this is too challenging, you can relax this, though note it may alter the narrative tenses that are used when reconstructing or noticed when comparing with the original.
- You can encourage students to create shorter texts by giving simply eight to ten key words/phrases, jumbled, and the opening line. The more "open to interpretation" the reconstruction becomes, the less chance there is of noticing certain forms when comparing with the original *but* the more scope there is for students to compare and evaluate each other group's work: they could vote on their favourite.
- Urban myths can be found easily through a google search. They are often dark, grim or taboo in nature so select carefully as appropriate to your class.

Language feedback options

- Narrative tenses, particularly the past perfect in contrast to the past simple (see many examples in the text – the fact that the phrases need to be used in order of appearance creates a need for the past perfect)
- The expressions/collocations from the pre-teach phase
- Time adverbials for sequencing the events – *earlier that day...later in the evening.*
- Sentence adverbials – *unsurprisingly*
- Subordinate/participle clauses – *putting them... crossing the back gardens... on turning the corner...*

▶ How to run the activity

Levels	B1–B2
Ages	all
Length	30–45 minutes

Materials	Worksheet 7d

Pre-task

- Board *Urban Myth/Urban Legend* and ask students to explain what it is. If they have no idea, tell them it's a kind of story and give a brief example:

> *a friend of a friend told me that once, a couple were walking by a river when they saw a small dog drowning. One of them jumped in a passed the dog to their partner. They took home the poor, wet, shivering animal, and wrapped it in a jumper. They decided to keep it – it didn't seem to have an owner (no collar). But when they arrived home, and the animal was dry, they realised it wasn't a dog. It was a…* (elicit/give the right answer – a very large rat).

Ask the students the following questions: *do they think this is true? Are urban myths usually true?* (Often not; sometimes there may be some truth there but the story has been exaggerated through many retellings). *Are they usually happy?* No – we tell them to feel better about our lives.

- Tell students they will be reconstructing an urban myth based on key words from the story. Give them worksheet 1, and ask them in small groups to look through the phrases. They should check their understanding of each phrase. Typically problematic items are: *to drown your sorrows, to have gambling debts, to stumble (home), to have a bright idea, to cover a crime* and *to sober up*.
- Once all the phrases are clear, point out to the students that the first and final sentences of the story have been given; and the others are listed <u>in the order that they appear</u> in the story. Tell them to take a couple of minutes to orally tell each other what they think the story is, based on this "skeleton".

Main task

- Using the upper section of the worksheet, students now work with the same partners to create their written version of the story, as the main task. Remind them: they should use the phrases in the order they appear; they should use all the phrases; they can add elements so their ideas "join together" better but should not add lots of extra details.
- As they write it up, monitor to check students are on task, and to help with any problems blocking the completion of the task.
- If a group finishes early, ask them to double check their story for accuracy and clarity. When all groups have finished, put each group with another group, and ask them to compare their stories, noticing any differences in the narrative.
- Give out the original urban myth. Ask them to read it and compare it with their own. Ask them to evaluate how similar their version is to the original (identical/very similar/quite different); ask them if they feel their version is better and why/why not.

7d Text reconstruction: Not his lucky day – your story

Complete the story in the empty box, using the phrases from the left in the same order they are listed.

Once, there was a man from Akron, Ohio who...

to have a disastrous day
a local bar
to drown (your) sorrows
earlier that day
to lose your job
to owe money
the local mafia
to get drunk
to stumble home
to have a bright idea
to break into a house
to steal valuables
to cover a crime
to set fire to something
to sober up
the horrible truth

It was his own house!

....

Now compare your story with the original. Which one is better and why? ☺

Once there was a man from Akron, Ohio, who'd had a disastrous day, so he went to his local bar to drown his sorrows. Earlier that day he'd lost in his job. He also had huge gambling debts with the local mafia. Unsurprisingly, perhaps, he got drunk. *Very* drunk. Later in the evening, he stumbled home. As he neared home, he had a bright idea – he crossed some dark gardens and broke into a house through a back window. He stole all the valuables he could find, putting them into a large suitcase he'd discovered. He decided to cover the crime by setting fire to the curtains in the living room. He then left the same way he came in, crossing the back gardens to the main road. On turning the corner into his own road, he instantly sobered up as he learned the horrible truth. He'd set fire to his own house.

ACTIVITIES FOR TASK-BASED LEARNING
by Neil Anderson and Neil McCutcheon

© DELTA Publishing, 2019 | www.deltapublishing.co.uk
ISBN 978-3-12-501701-6

7e Story jigsaw

 About the activity

Task type	problem-solving
Task outcome	Students recreate a story based on clues given.

Introduction

In some of our tasks, there is extensive pre-task preparation work – with visuals, discussion, pre-teaching and so on. That is not the case with this particular task – the students go into it deep end, as their goal is to find out what happened to the story-teller based on an opening line and the chance to ask a limited number of questions. The task involves minimal preparation but can last up to an hour: it is a good example of low preparation, high yield. A sample story is included below but ideally, you should find an equivalent that is true for you – the motivation of the students to find out what happened is much greater if they know it involves the suffering (or joy) of their teacher! I first heard of this task format from my former colleague Christopher Holmes.

Variation, extension, task repetition

- There are several options regarding the language focus: questions asked during Task 1 can be used for remedial work. If you are able to manage it, note any incorrect questions when asked on a slip of paper. Then, after Task 2 is complete, put these in a pile, asking each group to retrieve one at a time, then to attempt to improve/correct it.
- Groups can be asked to mine the transcript for any of the features mentioned in the language focus above. They can then look to compare something with their own output e.g. *what tenses did you use? Could you have used the past perfect or past continuous in your story? Where? Which adverbs could you use to make it more dramatic?*
- Groups could simply swap their written stories with each other, and offer peer correction in groups.

Language feedback options

- Question forms e.g. *why did you decide to go to the cake shop?*
- Narrative tenses e.g. *I looked around. No one had seen.*
- Informal spoken discourse markers e.g. *anyway… so… now… it turned out…*
- Adverbs for making a story more colourful/dramatic e.g. *seriously… immediately… incredibly.*
- Informal expressions e.g. *incredibly posh/posh prices… the lot… I'm not kidding… you know what's coming, right?… No way was I… walk of shame.*

▶ How to run the activity

Levels	▶ B1–C2
Ages	▶ 13+
Length	▶ 45–60 minutes

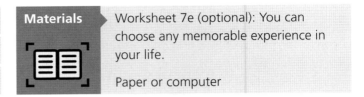

Materials ▶ Worksheet 7e (optional): You can choose any memorable experience in your life.

Paper or computer

Pre-task

- Put the opening sentence of the story on the board: *All I wanted was a croissant and a coffee, but I ended up with a headless chocolate bunny.*
- Tell the students the sentence on the board is the opening line of a story that happened to you (as noted, ideally, you will replace the sample with a real story about you: something out of the ordinary, whether scary, embarrassing or funny). Ask them if they think the story will be sad, happy, scary or embarrassing – in this case, it is the last.
- If you feel it will support the students, you can give some additional details e.g. the place and time of the story. However, it is important not to give away too much information as the aim of the task is to reconstruct a version of the story.

Task 1 (interrogation)

- Put the students into groups of three or four and set the task goal: they will have 5 minutes to ask you questions in order to find out more details of the story. At the end of this time, each group will write their story based on the first line and the information they have gathered by asking the teacher questions. Tell them that they will need to gather as much information as possible, and so their questions should be effective, using the information already gathered to find out more details of the events.
- Designate roles. One student in each group should be a *runner* – they need to come to you to ask the question, and then go back to report the answer (this role can be rotated); one will be a *secretary*, noting the answers to questions for the later reconstruction stage; and the others will take primary responsibility for thinking of the questions they ask you (however, all students should be involved in this). Tell the students you will answer with up to one or two lines of information before the runner has to return and report the answer for the secretary to note, and for the other students to use as the basis for a new question. It can help to model good/bad questions here; ask the students which of the following questions are more/less effective:
  - *So what happened to you?* (ineffective as too vague/open)
  - *Were you alone?* (ineffective as it is yes/no question and the answer will not be informative)
  - *Where were you and why were you there?* (effective as you can respond with one or two lines of information that should help generate the next question).
- Move yourself to some distance away from each group, and then give the signal to start. Groups should now think of their first question. When the runner comes to you, ensure this is done "one at a time", with runners from other groups out of earshot. Answer their questions and send them back to the group. It's important to be flexible here – you want each group to gather enough information to have a decent go at constructing the story; if you feel a group is not asking very useful questions, be less strict e.g. give them three or four lines of information, or prompt them regarding what they could ask about (e.g. *okay, so now you know I was in a cake shop – go back to the group and think of questions about what happened while I was there*).
  - Do this for *at least* 5 minutes – more if the groups still have energy and are thinking of questions.
  - One area for language focus later could be the questions they ask here – so make a note of any problems with question forms as you do this.

Task 2 (reconstruction and comparison)

- Ask the students if they think they have a decent idea of what happened. Tell them they should now give the story a title, and should reconstruct it, using *All I wanted was a croissant and a coffee, but I ended up with a headless chocolate bunny* as the opening line (the story can be told first person or third person, as they wish). They should include all the information they gathered and *also* should include one or two plausible lies in the story – something they did not hear from the teacher but that could have happened. Let them know they will be presenting their story later, so they should make it clear, logical and interesting.

- Give them 10 minutes to write the story up. Monitor and either help the students polish their stories by giving vocabulary/grammar, or make notes, saving this for subsequent language focus.

- When they have finished, tell each group to nominate a speaker, and bring them to the front of the class. Tell them to take turns to tell their story. The other groups should listen and try to identify the plausible lies (this can be harder than it seems as each group is likely to have gathered some details that differ from the other groups'). Tell them to make a note of the lies as they listen. Then, in feedback, check to see if managed to find the lies.

- Now tell them the full, true story: either play the audio file, or tell the story yourself. As the students listen, ask them to decide if the truth is more or less interesting than their own versions.

7e Story jigsaw – what you heard

Write the key information you hear:

Now write your final version of the story. Remember:

- you are going to read this to the other groups;
- you should include one or two lies in the story.

ACTIVITIES FOR TASK-BASED LEARNING
by Neil Anderson and Neil McCutcheon

© DELTA Publishing, 2019 | www.deltapublishing.co.uk
ISBN 978-3-12-501701-6

7e Story jigsaw – what the speaker said

All I wanted was a croissant and a coffee, but I ended up with a headless chocolate bunny. It was around Easter, and I was working in Zurich, Switzerland. Right next to the school was an incredibly posh cake shop – one that sold cakes, pastries, sandwiches, the lot. So we'd go there for snacks, though not every day, as the prices were posh too. Anyway, one day, I went in to get a croissant and a coffee. You know me – I'm a bit clumsy, and on this day, there was a large stand of chocolate bunnies near the end of the queue of customers. These were seriously high-end chocolate bunnies – I'm not kidding, wrapped in cellophane, with gold bows. Really expensive-looking. So, yes, I'm clumsy – you know what's coming, right? – as I moved forward in the queue, my arm knocked the display and all of a sudden, there was a shower of expensive chocolate bunnies raining down on me. Seriously. It was really embarrassing, though, this being Zurich, no one rushed to help or say anything, and the servers just ignored me. I felt like, incredibly, no one had noticed. So, anyway, I start picking up the five or six bunnies that had fallen, and carefully put them back in place. That's when I noticed – one of the bunnies had had a fatal accident. Its head had come clean off, and was just sitting there in the cellophane, detached from the body. I looked around. No one had seen. I checked the price and gasped as silently as I could – about 30 Swiss Francs, and I only had 20 on me. I immediately started sweating and, in my quiet panic, I'm ashamed to say I decided to hide the crime. As the queue moved I quietly placed the bunny behind some milk in an open fridge, and then waited for 5 minutes as I slowly, slowly moved to the head of the queue. I'd decided to just buy a croissant – no way was I waiting for coffee – and when I put it down, the lady at the till said something to me. Now, I wasn't long in Zurich, and my German wasn't great but it was something about the "kaputt" bunny. I pretended not to understand anything so she switched to English – "Sir, you will need to bring the broken bunny here and pay for it". Everyone stared at me as I did my walk of shame, back to the milky bunny grave, and then back again to the till, with the chocolate bunny limp in my hand. "Do you take cards? I don't have enough cash?" I asked. It turned out they didn't, so they marched me to a cash point on the busy street, as locals wondered why this red-faced foreigner was taking a headless bunny for a walk.

© DELTA Publishing, 2019 | www.deltapublishing.co.uk
ISBN 978-3-12-501701-6

ACTIVITIES FOR TASK-BASED LEARNING
by Neil Anderson and Neil McCutcheon

Additional resources

Are you a TBL teacher? – the quiz

Choose the answer, or answers, that best match your own beliefs and practice:

1. Which statement best captures your attitude to lesson planning?
   a. I plan very tightly so that there are "no hostages to fortune".
   b. I always structure my target language presentation carefully.
   c. I like to listen to students and react to their needs as much as possible.

2. Which of these best represents how you plan a series of lessons / scheme of work.
   a. After analysing my students' needs, I focus things in the real world that my students will be better able to do after the lessons.
   b. After analysing my students' needs, I focus on the grammar and lexis that my students are struggling with.
   c. I generally follow the contents pages of my course book, matched to the syllabus.

3. Which statement best captures your attitude to language practice?
   a. Controlled practice builds fluency; you learn a language in order to use it.
   b. Accuracy develops out of fluency; you use a language in order to learn it.
   c. It's important to have controlled and freer practice of the target language.

4. What are your beliefs about language learning?
   a. Explicit instruction is the most important process.
   b. Implicit learning is the most important process.
   c. No instruction is required.

5. What do you think about learners' errors?
   a. Their occurrence should be minimised, or – even better – avoided altogether.
   b. They are a natural part of a student's language development; I try to respond to them as they happen.
   c. I usually ignore them; they'll iron themselves out with time.

6. How do you approach task design?
   a. I often challenge students by throwing them "in at the deep end" with little guidance.
   b. I think it's worthwhile providing some preparation for the task.
   c. I never let students use language that hasn't been well rehearsed beforehand.

ACTIVITIES FOR TASK-BASED LEARNING
by Neil Anderson and Neil McCutcheon

© DELTA Publishing, 2019 | www.deltapublishing.co.uk
ISBN 978-3-12-501701-6

Are you a TBL Teacher? – the key

Choose the answer, or answers, that best match your own beliefs and practice:

7. Which statement best captures your attitude to lesson planning?
    d. I plan very tightly so that there are "no hostages to fortune". **1 point**
    e. I always structure my target language presentation carefully. **2 points**
    f. I like to listen to students and react to their needs as much as possible. **3 points**

    Of course there is nothing wrong with a well-structured lesson, but TBL is a more student-centred methodology, in which their needs will help determine the language agenda – and so you should end up having to plan less.

8. Which of these best represents how you plan a series of lessons / scheme of work.
    d. After analysing my students' needs, I focus things in the real world that my students will be better able to do after the lessons. **3 points**
    e. After analysing my students' needs, I focus on the grammar and lexis that my students are struggling with. **1 point**
    f. I generally follow the contents pages of my course book, matched to the syllabus. **0 points**

    A task-based syllabus should ideally be based on students' needs, and focus on tasks that they need to do. This is also called an analytic syllabus because it is not organised around a series of pre-selected structures or lexis. A Needs Analysis is obviously good to do in all cases.

9. Which statement best captures your attitude to language practice?
    d. Controlled practice builds fluency; you learn a language in order to use it. **2 points**
    e. Accuracy develops out of fluency; you use a language in order to learn it. **3 points**
    f. It's important to have controlled and freer practice of the target language. **1 point**

    Task-Based Learning is a fluency first approach; the key driver of language learning is students trying to mean things, and this determines their choice of language forms. (Of course, there is some value in most kinds of language practice, especially when this is meaningful in some way.)

10. What are your beliefs about language learning?
    d. Explicit instruction is the most important process. **1 point**
    e. Implicit learning is the most important process. **3 points**
    f. No instruction is required. **2 points**

    Implicit learning is the default process, and it is a legitimate criticism of many teacher training courses that they do not recognise this, or communicate it sufficiently to trainees. Instruction in a language isn't strictly necessary, but it is usually useful and can speed up the process. Explicit attention to language forms appears to help build implicit knowledge – by a process that is not yet wholly understood.

© DELTA Publishing, 2019 | www.deltapublishing.co.uk
ISBN 978-3-12-501701-6

ACTIVITIES FOR TASK-BASED LEARNING
by Neil Anderson and Neil McCutcheon

Are you a TBL teacher? – the key

11. What do you think about learners' errors?
   d. Their occurrence should be minimised, or – even better – avoided altogether.   0 points
   e. They are a natural part of a student's language development; I try to respond to them as they happen.   3 points
   f. I usually ignore them; they'll iron themselves out with time.   2 points

Errors are a natural – and unavoidable – part of interlanguage development. Nor should they be avoided; mistakes aren't a bad thing. Mistakes can provide opportunities for students to negotiate meaning and for teachers to focus on form (implicitly through recasts, or in explicit clarification.) They indicate that students are prepared to take risks and push the boundaries of what they know, a strong predictor for success in language learning.

12. How do you approach task design?
   d. I often challenge students by throwing them "in at the deep end" with little guidance.   2 points
   e. I think it's worthwhile providing some preparation for the task.   3 points
   f. I never let students use language that hasn't been well rehearsed beforehand.   0 points

See various of the points above. The essence of TBL is getting students to communicate in a second language and to attempt to encode meaning independently. Students may well perform better on tasks where these are scaffolded by adequate preparation, such as participating in pre-task activities, and being exposed to texts.

13–18 points:	**You already follow a number of the key principles of TBL and would have little problem wading deeper into a fluency first approach.**
6–12 points:	**You are a principled teacher who has a flexible approach to your practice. You should be able to dip your toe into the water of TBL, though it may feel a little disorientating at first.**
0–5 points:	**You prefer to be in control of the language agenda, and to follow a more linear lesson format. You could try out some of the ideas in this book as "freer practice" to begin with.**

ACTIVITIES FOR TASK-BASED LEARNING
by Neil Anderson and Neil McCutcheon

© DELTA Publishing, 2019 | www.deltapublishing.co.uk
ISBN 978-3-12-501701-6

DELTA Publishing

Sample Consciousness-Raising worksheet for 5a Nostalgia story

This is an example of a CR worksheet we might use after a **focused task**, with the intention of helping learners notice a more limited or specific language area. Here, the area is past simple, *used to* and *would* for past habits and states. **A** involves recognizing the forms in the text / transcript; **B** focuses attention on the different functions of the relevant structures; **C** looks at how they are used in discourse (used to tends to start new topics, and the other forms provide details).

A: What three verb forms did I use to talk about the past?
Tick ✓ them if you can find an example in the sample text:

the past simple	the past perfect	used to + infinitive
had + infinitive	would + infinitive	the past continuous

B: Look at the examples in the text. Which form do we use for which meaning?
Tick ✓ the box whenever it is true:

	Past simple	Used to	Would
Past states			
Repeated past actions			
Past actions that happened only once			

C:
When telling nostalgia stories, which form do we use for introducing new topics?
Which forms do we use to give more information / details?

ACTIVITIES FOR TASK-BASED LEARNING
by Neil Anderson and Neil McCutcheon

Glossary of key terms

accuracy	The degree to which a learner's language is recognised as correct because it conforms to the norms of the relevant speech community to which he/she belongs, including proficient speakers of English as an international language (EIL). In learning contexts, this variable is often contrasted with both *fluency* and linguistic *complexity.*
affordances	Opportunities for language learning within the learner's environment. The term is associated with the view of language development as a complex organic system which responds to feedback, as described by Diane Larsen-Freeman.
chunks	Associated with a lexical view of language, chunks are units of *formulaic language* which can be learned as wholes and contribute towards a learner's *fluency.* Chunks include sentence stems, collocations, colligations, fixed and semi-fixed expressions, and polywords such as compounds and multi-word verbs.
consciousness-raising (C-R) activities	These are learner-centred language-focused activities which encourage learners to explore the relationship between language forms and meaning, by paying attention to examples. These can be contrasted with a more didactic teacher-led approach focused on rules.
distributed practice	This refers to a focus on specific language forms which is spread over time rather than *massed* i.e. concentrated into one lesson.
emergent language	In pedagogy, the kind of language that arises in the performance of a task, in contrast to language that has been pre-selected by the teacher. This may refer to language that is produced by the learners themselves, or is provided as support by the teacher. (This is different from the theory of *emergence* in complex systems such as mind.)
expansions	This occurs in language feedback and correction, when the teacher adds words, for example ellipted words, to make the meaning clearer. Mike Long mentions that texts can be simplified in this way by a process he calls *elaborated input.*
explicit learning (instruction)	This is conscious learning – when learners' attention is focused on language form as a result of direct teaching, or by means of an exercise, or through self-study. One principle of TBL is that the effects of this kind of learning are often overestimated. It increases the store of *explicit knowledge* i.e. knowledge *about* language.
feedback	This is information about a learner's performance given by another person such as the teacher. It can be *explicit* or *implicit,* and *immediate* or *delayed.* **Content feedback** focuses on the substance of the task; **process feedback** on the experience of completing the task. It is commonly (though not universally) accepted that one of the teacher's essential roles is to provide **language feedback**.
feedback templates	Blank forms and tables included in this book to help structure language feedback.
flash reading	A procedure in which students are allowed to look at a text for a very brief period of time, before the text is hidden, and students recall as much information as they can from their short-term memory. This may be repeated several times, depending on the length and complexity of the text.
fluency first approach	Also called *fluency-led* or *fluency-to-accuracy,* this describes a deep communicative approach to language learning (such as TBL, DOGME, content-based teaching or CLL) where the meaning of what is said is prioritised over attention to language form. This contrasts with more form-focused approaches such as PPP.

focused tasks (or focused communication task)	This is a kind of task where a specific language focus has been pre-selected and made prominent because it will inevitably arise during the performance of the task. This language focus should not distract students' attention from the meaning of the task, however.
focus on form (FonF)	This is when learners' attention is drawn to language forms, especially through correction, including *recasts*. In TBL, it is by definition *reactive* and happens after learners have been exposed to language in context, and usually in the latter stages of a lesson following the task itself.
grammaticise	Transforming key words into a grammatically standard, fully coherent text. Grammaticisation is the process students engage with in **text reconstruction** activities.
ICE – identify, capture, exploit	The steps needed to effectively deal with emergent language. The teacher needs to be in a position to notice learner output (*identify*), make notes for subsequent feedback (*capture*) and be prepared to clarify and practise relevant identified and captured language (*exploit*).
implicit learning	This is learning in which a learner is not aware that learning is taking place. It leads to *implicit knowledge,* not always easy or possible to articulate, which is the kind of knowledge associated with *skills* such as mastery of a sport or musical instrument – or a language. TBL practitioners acknowledge that it is the most important process involved in language learning.
incidental learning	This is learning that happens when the learner is paying attention to something other than the language itself. This is how children learn their first language.
intentional learning	Deliberate learning, such as when a learner is preparing for an examination by memorising a list of grammar rules or vocabulary items.
interlanguage	Coined by Selinker, L (1972), this is a concept which describes a learner's continually developing (and internally consistent) representation of the target language. Knowledge of different structures develops at different rates and, according to SLA theory, in a relatively predictable order, on which language teaching has little long-term influence.
meta-analysis	A synthesis of a large number of published research studies.
negotiation of meaning	The process of interlocutors working to understand each other clearly when engaged in e.g. problem-solving or information gap tasks. This can be done through seeking clarification, reformulating what one has said as well as numerous other strategies. Research suggests it provides optimal conditions for acquiring new language as attention is focused on both meaning and form.
noticing	The cognitive process of a learner becoming aware of new language (whether grammar or lexis) that was previously not salient to them. A related idea is when learners **notice the gap** i.e. are able to compare the difference between their own current output and a target model they are exposed to. Noticing is considered to be an important trigger for acquisition as it facilitates the conversion of input to intake. Post-task language focus and techniques such as recasts are designed to maximise the potential for noticing. The "noticing hypothesis" was originally proposed by Richard Schmidt.
proceduralisation	See **skill-building theory**.

recasts	When a teacher (or another student) immediately repeats an upgraded/corrected version of student output back to them e.g. S: "I felt myself well at the party" T: "You mean… *I had a good time at the party*". Because the student is invested in the exchange, the recast creates the potential for noticing new language.
scaffolding	The support a teacher offers a learner as they try to express themselves, complete a task, or **proceduralise** language use. This could be given through explicit guidance, affective support, the provision of input, thinking and preparation time, or other means. Typically scaffolding is gradually "removed" (lessened) as the learner masters the task or skill.
schema/ta	Theoretical knowledge stored in the mind containing the sum of an individual's background knowledge and experience of a concept. Schema can be classed in various ways, including **content schema** (knowledge of topics) and **formal schema** (knowledge of rhetorical structures in discourse, such as genre conventions). Schema activation is an important part of pre-task preparation.
sentence stems	A type of **chunk** providing a formulaic, functional opening to a sentence e.g. *It's useful for…* This is then completed by the contextually relevant referential information e.g. *It's useful for* keeping track of the time.
skill-building theory	The idea that mastery of a language involves progressing through various stages, such as a) becoming aware of language rules and items, through to b) more conscious, controlled processing of language before c) enjoying more automatic use; when knowledge of language is **proceduralised** in this way, it can be used readily and accurately without requiring much processing capacity.
spiral	A type of syllabus where topics, tasks and language items are repeated across the course. There is typically an increase in complexity when the item is returned to.
structure-based syllabus	An example of a **synthetic syllabus** where the language is broken down into constituent parts (in this case, grammatical structures), and is then ordered along the lines of perceived difficulty e.g. 1st conditional is taught before 2nd conditional. A task-based syllabus by contrast is **analytic** as content is not organised through pre-selected and specifically graded language items but in terms of the communicative purposes language is used for.
syntactic complexity	In task performance, the degree to which learners attend more to accurate use of language, and in particular which structures to use in order to express what they wish to communicate more precisely. Factors such as preparation/thinking time, awareness of having an audience and task repetition can increase syntactic complexity in learner output.
syntactic processing	Analysing a sentence in terms of the word order and roles of the words within the sentence; thinking about the accurate use of grammatical structures and word grammar (colligation).
task feedback	This is the specific information and evaluation given by a teacher (or peer) immediately after the completion of a task. See **feedback** for more.
task goal	Also known as **task outcome**, it provides learners with a reason to focus on **negotiate of meaning** during the completion of a task. For example, learners may be asked to *identify differences between two versions of a story*, with each learner telling one version and the other listening.
text reconstruction	A type of task which involves as part of its procedure the reassembly of a text from key words. The reconstructed text is then compared to the original and learners are encouraged to **notice the gap** between their version and the original.

Index

Grammar

Articles 7a
Both/neither 4d
Comparatives and superlatives 2b, 2c, 2f, 3f, 5e
Conditionals (real) 3c, 5d, 5g
Conditionals (unreal) 2d, 5f
Discourse markers 3b, 3e, 7e
Focusing adverbs *(in fact, actually)* 3e
For/since 6a
Future perfect 3f
Imperative 5h
Infinitive of purpose 5d, 5g
Linking words 2c, 3e, 4b, 7c
Modal verbs 2a, 2f, 3c, 3d, 3f, 3g, 4b, 6e
Narrative tenses 5c, 5f, 7a, 7d, 7e
Participle clauses 2e, 3f, 4c, 5d, 7b, 7c, 7d
Passive 2a, 2c, 3f, 3g, 6f
Past simple tense 3g, 4e, 5a
Past continuous 5c
Prepositional phrases 4c
Present perfect 4e, 5e, 5f, 6a
Present simple 2c, 4a, 6c
Present continuous 4a, 4c
Quantifiers 2f, 5h
Question forms 4c, 4e, 7e
Relative clauses 2e, 4c, 5d, 7b
Reported speech 4a, 4d
Sequencing adverbs 5f, 5h, 6c, 6d, 7b,
There is/there are 4c
Time adverbials 5c, 5e, 5h, 7d
Used to 3g, 5a
Would for past habit 5a

Lexis / functions

Achievements 5e
Advice 3c, 5g
Animals 2c, 7c
Anti-social behaviour/annoying habits 4a
Appearance 3g
Art 6e
Business idea 6f
Certainty 4b, 5g
Coincidences 5f
Counselling 3c
Crime 2a, 7d
Describing people and places 4c
Fame 5e
Fashion 3g
Films 6c
Feelings 5b
Flatmates 2f, 4a
Food 5h
Friends 5f
Generalising 2c, 3e
Hairstyles 3g
Health 5g
Heroes 5e
Hotels 6d
Houses and flats 6b
Hypotheticals 2d, 5f
Impressions 6c, 6e
Interviews 6a
Journalists 6a
Landlords 3d, 4a, 6b
Legal language 2a
Lies 4e
Likes and dislikes *(love, don't mind, can't stand)* 2b, 2d, 2e
Marketing 6f
Medicine 5g

Memories 5b
Music 5b, 6a
Neighbours 2e, 4a
Neighbourhoods/local areas 2e, 6b
Obligation 3a, 3c
Opinions 2a, 3b, **3e*,** 4a, 4b, 5e, 6e
Parents and children 3a
Permission 3a, 3c
Personality 2f, 3c, 3g, 5e
Persuading 6b, 6e
Polite requests 3d
Preferences 2b, 3g, 4d
Probability 7c
Recipes 5h
Remember/remind 5b
Rules and regulations 3a
Scepticism 4b
Similarities and differences 2c, 4d
Speculation 4b, 6c, 6e
Songs 5b
Suggestions (Recommendations) 3c, 5g, 6b, 6d
Technology 3f, 5d
Tenants 3d, 4a, 6b
Usefulness 3f
Youth 3g

***You can find the main list of functional exponents for expressing opinions in 3b.**

References

Arnold, J. Murphey, T. (2013). *Meaningful Action: Earl Stevick's Influence on Language Teaching.* Cambridge, UK: Cambridge University Press.

Arnold, J. Dörnyei, Z. Pugliese, C. (2015) *The Principled Communicative Approach: Seven Criteria for Success* London, UK: Helbling Languages.

Chaudron (1988). *Second Language Classrooms: Research on teaching and learning.* Cambridge, UK: Cambridge University Press

Conti G. (2018). *Patterns First – How I Teach Lexicogrammar.* Retrieved from https://gianfrancoconti.wordpress.com/2018/07/30/patterns-first-how-i-teach-lexicogrammar-part-1/

Csikszentmihaly, Mihaly https://positivepsychologyprogram.com/mihaly-csikszentmihalyi-father-of-flow/#flow-types-characteristics

Doughty C. & Williams J (eds.). (1998). *Focus On Form in Classroom Second Language Acquisition.* Cambridge, UK: Cambridge University Press.

Edge, J. (1986). "Acquisition disappears in adultery": interaction in the translation class. *ELT Journal, 40*(2), 121–124.

Ellis, R. Nobuyoshi, J. (1993). Focused communication tasks and second language acquisition. *ELT Journal, 47*(3), 203–210.

Ellis, R. (2015). *Understanding Second Language Acquisition (2nd edition).* Oxford, UK: Oxford University Press.

Finocchiaro, M., Brumfit, C. (1983). *The functional-notional approach: from theory to practice.* New York, USA: Oxford University Press.

Foster, P. Snyder Ohta, A. (2006). Negotiation for Meaning and Peer Assistance in Second Language Classrooms. *Applied Linguistics 26*(3), 402–430.

Hendra, L. A. & Jones, C. (2018). *Motivating learners with immersive speaking tasks:* Part of the Cambridge Papers in ELT series. Cambridge, UK: Cambridge University Press.

Hoey M. (2005). *Lexical Priming.* Abingdon, UK: Routledge.

Kerr, P. (2017). *Giving feedback on speaking.* Part of the Cambridge Papers in ELT series. Cambridge, UK: Cambridge University Press.

Klippel, F. (1984). *Keep Talking.* Cambridge, UK: Cambridge University Press

Larsen-Freeman, D. (2003). *From Grammar to Grammaring.* Heinle ELT.

Li, S., Ellis, R., & Zhu, Y. (2016). Task-based versus task-supported language instruction: An experimental study. *Annual Review of Applied Linguistics, 36*, 205–229.

Long, M. (2015). *Second Language Acquisition and Task-based Language Teaching* Chichester: Wiley.

Long, M. (2016). In Defense of Tasks and TBLT: Nonissues and Real Issues. *Annual Review of Applied Linguistics, 36*, 5–33. Cambridge, UK: Cambridge University Press

Maley, A. interview with Dr N.S. Prabhu, *The Teacher Trainer* –Saved from: https://www.tttjournal.co.uk/uploads/File/back_articles/Interview_with_Dr_Prabhu.pdf

Nation I.S.P. (2013). *Learning Vocabulary in Another Language.* Cambridge, UK: Cambridge University Press.

Nunan, D. (2004). *Task-Based Language Teaching.* Cambridge, UK: Cambridge University Press.

Prabhu, N. S. (1987). *Second Language Pedagogy.* Oxford: Oxford University Press.

Selinker, L. (1972) *Interlanguage. International Review of Applied Linguistics*, 10: 209-31

Skehan, P. (1998). *A Cognitive Approach to Language Learning.* Oxford, UK: Oxford University Press.

Skehan, P. (2003). *Task-Based Instruction. Language Teaching 36*(1), 1–14.

Thornbury, S. (2017). *30 Language Teaching Methods.* Cambridge, UK: Cambridge University Press.

Thornbury, S. (2009). Slow-release grammar *English Teaching Professional, 61*, 4–6.

Thornbury, S. (1997). Reformulation and reconstruction: tasks that promote "noticing". *ELT Journal 51*(4), 326–335.

Thornbury, S.(2013) *The Learning Body in Meaningful Action*. Cambridge, UK: Cambridge University Press

Willis, D. *Focus on Meaning, Language and Form: a Three Way Distinction*. Retrieved from http://www.willis-elt.co.uk/articles-dave-willis/

Willis, J. (1996). *A Framework For Task-Based Learning*. Harlow, UK: Longman.

Willis, D. & Willis, J. (2007). *Doing Task-Based Teaching: A practical guide to task-based teaching for ELT training courses and practising teachers*. Oxford, UK: Oxford University Press.

Willis, D. & Willis, J. (eds.) (1996). *Challenge & Change in Language Teaching* Oxford, UK: Macmillan Heinemann.

Further reading

If you would like to read more about TBL (TBLT), we recommend the following books.

The most accessible and practical book for beginners is Jane Willis's original formulation of TBL, *A Framework For Task-Based Learning* (1996).

Post-initial training, teachers will find *Challenge & Change in Language Teaching* edited by Jane and Dave Willis (1996) very useful. This is a collection of several short, readable articles on TBL versus PPP; the lexical approach; consciousness-raising and teacher development, in some cases by the authors with whom these ideas originated.

The definitive book on TBL for experienced teachers is Mike Long's *Second Language Acquisition And Task-Based Language Teaching* (2015). This is the culmination of a lifetime's work in the field of Second Language Acquisition. Long describes the psycholinguistic underpinnings of the approach in depth, as well as setting it within a broader humanist tradition of education. The book contains comprehensive discussions of Needs Analysis, task design and discourse analysis.

Peter Skehan's 1998 book, *A Cognitive Approach to Language Learning* focuses in particular on two systems: rule-based and exemplar-based language. He discusses how tasks can be designed in order to cater to these dual modes of psycholinguistic processing.

For a summary of the most recent research, read "TBLT implementation and evaluation: A meta-analysis" by Bryfonski and McKay in Language Teaching Research (2017).

Photos